SpringerBriefs in Education

More information about this series at http://www.springer.com/series/8914

Christine Angela Eastman

Improving Workplace Learning by Teaching Literature

Towards Wisdom

 Springer

Christine Angela Eastman
Hendon, London
UK

ISSN 2211-1921   ISSN 2211-193X   (electronic)
SpringerBriefs in Education
ISBN 978-3-319-29026-3   ISBN 978-3-319-29028-7   (eBook)
DOI 10.1007/978-3-319-29028-7

Library of Congress Control Number: 2016935596

Printed on acid-free paper

This Springer imprint is published by Springer Nature
The registered company is Springer International Publishing AG Switzerland

Foreword

The UK banking industry currently faces a number of challenges, not least rebuilding trust among consumers. Halifax Community Bank, as part of Lloyds Banking Group, is totally committed to this, and our ability to deliver consistently fair outcomes for customers is central to our vision of being the best bank for customers.

We recognise that if we are to meet the needs and expectations of our customers now and in the future we need to continue to work closely with all employees to build and develop a diverse and inclusive team. It is a smart organisation which recognises the knowledge its employees have is where its true wealth lies. Investing in training and development, providing colleagues with the tools and capabilities they need to do their job well and making a difference to customers are key.

It is not something that all banks would be comfortable doing, but encouraging colleagues to think critically about current banking practice and suggesting ways the bank can improve to benefit the business as a whole makes us stand out. Not only does it encourage the right people to want to come and work with us, but also it reinforces confidence in the bank.

We want to become the best bank for colleagues as well as for customers. Our aim is to build a culture where our core values underpin everything we do, but if this is to happen we need to take colleagues outside the branch and give them the tools and the environment to develop the skill of critical thinking. Applying this to the bank and how it works for the benefit of customers is sound management practice; you cannot change a culture through a top-down approach alone.

Since 2010, over 400 Halifax bank managers have completed the Advanced Diploma in Retail Banking Practice, and we are the first bank to have a fully qualified branch manager workforce on the high street.

Choosing the right course was really important to us. Some colleagues have no prior academic background or have been out of education for a good number of years, so we didn't want this to be another conventional, prescriptive, tick-box employee training course. We wanted the focus to be on educating colleagues to become creative and critical thinkers, and believe this innovative approach of integrating literature into a work-based learning curriculum achieves this. Christine Eastman's book *Improving Workplace Learning by Teaching Literature* details how learners can become more creative and critical thinkers, and the cornerstone chapter on working with the Halifax could serve as a blueprint for other retail banks and organisations in the wider world of commerce to support their employees to shape the direction of their companies.

A key tenet of the course is helping colleagues implement a structured training process for all existing customer advisers within their branch. This helps us to support their personal development but at the same time moves us towards the goal of having all customer queries dealt with at first point of contact. One measure of how this has proved successful has been the drop in the number of complaints against the bank. We now have half the number you'd expect to see for a big bank, and our branch managers have had a big role in this, many of whom have now taken this course.

Other colleagues who have taken the course have seen their external research influence the bank's business decisions and can say they have directly shaped the future of the bank. As more colleagues benefit from the certificate it is proving to be a real motivational factor for other colleagues who can see, first-hand, how they are making a real difference for their colleagues and customers.

Not all banks will do this or will be brave enough to encourage critical, independent thinking but that is what makes us different. We are seeing the benefits in terms of increased customer numbers and in attracting people of this mindset to want to come and work with us.

David Nicholson
Group Director, Halifax Community Bank

Contents

Chapter 1
Introduction

Abstract The introduction to Improving Workplace Learning by Teaching Literature: Towards Wisdom explains the use of students' stories as a way of examining the experience of working with different organisations and individuals. It also explains the book's several purposes: to provide educators with ideas on how to integrate literature into a work based curriculum; to encourage companies to help their employees become creative and critical thinkers through reading widely; to offer anyone interested in education insights and practical ideas on how a marriage between pragmatic problem solving and reading literature can be effected. The companies illustrated in the book are those that encourage their employees to articulate their knowledge and make their insights available to their organisation. The smart organisation recognises that the knowledge its employees have is where its true wealth lies, and that knowledge can be revealed through inspiring education. The introduction introduces the reader to the book's mission: there is a pressing need to introduce literature and students' stories into a business based curriculum.

This is a book about stories, mainly about students' stories, but other stories are woven into the narrative of five case studies about using literature in a work based learning curriculum. This book could have been a "how to" guide on how to teach and how to help students extract relevant information from their reading. A "how to" guide in itself would have been a worthwhile project, but instead I wanted to use the students' stories as a prism through which to examine my own experiences of working with different organisations and individuals. I wanted to narrate a story of how I encourage students to find their own voices. My teaching career has taught me that if I was able to develop strong, confident voices in my students, they would be able to articulate their own stories. Furthermore, through examining powerful voices in literature, reflecting on how these voices succeed in the transmission of their message and developing their own voices as a result of these explorations, students gain in confidence and truly begin the process of transformative learning. The book has several purposes. The first is to provide educators with ideas on how to integrate literature into a work based learning curriculum. The second is to

© The Author(s) 2016
C.A. Eastman, *Improving Workplace Learning by Teaching Literature*,
SpringerBriefs in Education, DOI 10.1007/978-3-319-29028-7_1

encourage companies to help their employees become creative and critical thinkers through reading widely. A third purpose is to offer to anyone interested in education—students, teachers, managers, industry leaders, curriculum developers— insights and practical ideas on how a marriage between pragmatic problem solving and reading literature can be effected.

In *Making Stories: Law, Literature, Life* (2002: 3) Jerome Bruner asks the reader if another book "about narrative, about stories, what they are and how they are used" is needed. Through a rich range of examples drawn from Freudian analysis to the US Supreme Court's anti-segregation ruling, from the Book of Genesis to the innovative programme in narrative medicine at Columbia University's School of Medicine, Bruner demonstrates that the sheer force of the ideas inherent in stories changes lives by telling us about ourselves, by giving us "access to the culture's treasury of stories" (100). As a psychologist, Bruner is interested in the potency of narrative to illuminate meaning-making, alternative worlds and possibilities and, above all, language. My foray into using literature in a work based curriculum was motivated by my concern with students' inability to articulate what they wanted to write. Their struggle with the English language not only dismayed me but also suggested to me a link between their incapacity to construct a coherent narrative with a worrying lack of confidence, even a lack of sense of self. Too often, the bright and inquiring students who wrestle with the mechanics of grammar are invariably the same students who feel they have been held back professionally by not being able to use language with ease. Recently, one of my students, a director of his own successful manufacturing franchise, admitted "I'm starting to use words and expressions I never thought I would—the kind `brainy solicitor types' use." Thinking and writing differently can take students out of their comfort zone, as the cliché goes: broadening the mind is challenging, destabilising, alienating even. This same student went on to read at my suggestion Neill Ferguson's *High Financier: Lives and Time of Siegmund Warburg* because he was intrigued by the origins of globalisation and the history of finance. Was the experience worth it? "I learnt new expressions—haute banque, martinet, tableaux, Russophobic," he reeled off, "Some of the book bored me but I was fascinated by the language." As Bruner points out, self-telling may proceed in ordinary language, yet lexical exploration reflects a sharp willingness to learn and a profound turning point in self-narration.

I was further compelled to write this book because of an experience I had recently with a well known UK based training organisation. In an all day seminar, a group of department heads, people in human resources, managers, educators—anyone interested in the topic of "leadership"—were subjected to over 30 slides of leadership "models" on familiar stalwarts such as Stephen Covey and James Scouller. More than an hour was devoted to the Honey and Mumford learning inventory: raise your hand if you are an activist! Are there any reflectors in the audience? In her defence, the self-styled facilitator mentioned that much of what she was going through— learning styles in particular—had been somewhat discredited in recent years, but I kept thinking—then why are we spending £500 and giving up a day to debate in small groups who liked or didn't like to take the initiative in awkward situations? The workshop was not inspiring but rather cynical, banal and distinctly dispiriting.

It made me reflect on the fact that thousands of employees all over the UK are subjected to precisely this type of experience in the name of some notional idea of "educating" one's workforce:

> The difference between corporate training and real education – what we have here – is that with corporate training, people come in, give you a massive folder of stuff and expect you to work through it. Whereas with this university course, you get a few pages, read them in depth and reflect on them. There's more essence; there's more to it than a training course.

This Toshiba student perceives that a training company, briefed by an organisation, imposes its ideas on what they think employees need in order to improve their practice. I had experienced generic "training" and remained unconvinced of its merits. I have come to value the rare, enlightened organisation like Toshiba that realises that its own employees have the most knowledge about the organisation. Such employees are encouraged to articulate their knowledge and can then make their insights available to their organisation: it is employee *education* rather than employee *training* that should be the focus of every business. The smart organisation recognises that the knowledge its employees have is where its true wealth lies, and that knowledge can be revealed through inspiring education.

Naturally it is essential to discover what "inspiring" education looks like. Within a work based learning curriculum at the Institute of Work Based Learning at Middlesex University I have been endeavouring to introduce the humanities, mainly in the form of American and English literature, to students to help them address the challenges of their working lives by thinking more deeply and reflectively. My own background as a lecturer in English and American literature has enabled me to introduce students to literary culture as well as help them to use the textual power of well crafted literature to express themselves precisely. In the chapters that follow I aim to demonstrate what inspiring education looks like: you will read the accounts of students who have encountered a range of literature, which they have integrated into their own academic writing, to make it as original, effective and rigorous as possible. Students have been able to mine literature to understand better their own lives and relationships with others. Working with individual students or with students in business cohorts, I have always promoted the Wildean adage that to know everything about oneself, one must know all about others.[1] The book is divided in the following way.

Chapter 2 looks at the work I did with ToshibaTEC. In the spring of 2011 I began to work with a half dozen students from the ToshibaTEC corporation in Chertsey, Surrey because the company wanted to effect a culture of transformation. The company was looking for an alternative to staff development through appraisals as well as to introduce changes to improve performance. Students were expected to examine the challenges of staff behaviour and performance in order to drive change within their own environments. Drawing on essays by Ron Barnett, Robert Coles and work on wisdom by Anne Kinsella and Allan Pitman I demonstrate how I used both academic literature and literary essays to help students learn more about work

---

[1] Oscar Wilde's (1891) "The Critic as Artist" *Intentions*. London: James R Osgood McIlvaine.

and themselves. I designed a programme to encourage them to read widely—to get them accustomed to exploring literature, which was and has always been my primary goal with work based learning students.

I wanted to support them to develop their voices, to articulate their positions in the workplace, to consolidate their authority, to project their "selves". Through literature students can reflect on and examine their social values such as cultural awareness. They can look at each other's stories to help them to reflect on their own values. I introduced James Baldwin's "Notes of a Native Son" (1984), a powerful testimony of racism, which I thought far stronger than any kind of training course on "recognising diversity and the importance of cultural awareness". Baldwin's voice is fashioned into an argument in which personal experience is used evidentially to illustrate a specific position, in this case someone marginalised and persecuted by racist attitudes. I wanted students to examine Baldwin's style and use of voice as he invests a personal experience with political significance. Baldwin could tutor the students in using an intimate voice to engage politically, thereby demonstrating to them the importance of voice in conveying messages: the personal is invariably political.

Reflection is the cornerstone of work based learning, a reflection that I maintain is nurtured by literature that creates that breakthrough moment, that clear vision of other lives and other scenarios, that new way of seeing. Often students are worried about what they have got themselves "into" with a daunting programme of academic study. Examining powerful voices in literature helps students to produce prose that has a "voice": ultimately literature can support students in making a more substantial contribution to their organisations.

Fortuitiously, I am back working with Toshiba again, this time with executive managers on an MSc in Sales Leadership. Before they come to me, they are introduced to a range of sales incentives and motivational models and are perfectly comfortable discussing the GROW model, the conceptualisation of value-based selling or the finer points of Action Research. However, I got a sense that they hadn't shaped their stories yet, that some of their subversive spirits hadn't been tapped. My introducing them to Henry David Thoreau was prompted by a discussion I had with them about identifying personal values that shape their everyday experiences and then showcasing these values meaningfully in their writing. Thoreau's poignant explanation for withdrawing to the Concord wood, "I wanted to live deep and suck at the marrow of life, to live so sturdily and Spartan-like as to put to rout all that was not life, to cut a broad swathe and shove close, to drive life into a corner, and reduce it to its lowest terms, and, if it proved mean, why then to get the whole and genuine meanness to the world; or if it were sublime, to know it by experience, and to be able to give a true account of it" (2007: 1920) perhaps resonated with them as salespeople because by their own accounts they are hard-pressed by the exigencies of the rapid and demanding world of selling, finding it difficult to carve out the time to reflect, to paraphrase Thoreau on the "phenomena" of their lives. As an MSc in sales leadership student pointed out: "His words are thrusting and strong—he means business and he means to sell his idea to his readers. He is committed and dedicated to testing his principles and is right about living without such hurry and waste of life. He is not merely telling us, but making us share the experience. If we can help our teams close the gap between telling and showing as well as avoiding what isn't important we'll be half-way there."

Chapter 3 discusses my time with a group of security managers selected from among the team responsible for hundreds of security and steward staff at Wembley Stadium. These students, who managed highly pressurised situations involving the public safety of up to 95,000 people including employees and spectators, were expected to create positive change by focusing on the theme of leadership. I aimed to instil authority in the students by encouraging them to read widely in the field of leadership theory. I also introduced them to 19th century essayists to test whether more "literary" literature would be helpful for their learning. I provided them with essays from Francis Bacon and George Eliot in order to illustrate the mechanics of constructing an argument. I found that students were able to demonstrate that they could move beyond citing examples of individuals who they thought were good leaders to be able to analyse the concept of leadership itself. For example, using Francis Bacon's essay on revenge to examine what makes a great leader provided a richness to their arguments. They were able to apply knowledge derived from literary works produced by the greatest thinkers to their current practice as well as to grasp the ethical aspects of leadership such as discerning the difference between "leadership" and "good leadership".

I emphasised the techniques of close reading, asking students to examine texts in fine detail so that their narratives would start to take on a degree of criticality. Moreover, I encouraged them to use a narrative approach to re-define problems because of my belief that we use stories to make sense of our experiences and that much of creativity lies in storytelling. The students were able to recognise the power of rhetoric, of being able to use language with precision and cogency, to question all matters critically. It was important for them to learn how to express their rejection of stale, conventional thinking as clearly as possible.

Chapter 3 is concerned more broadly with the examination of a transformation of self, in which I argue that the investiture into university needs to be *from* work: the university should find more of their students from a pool of those already working, already exposed to corporate life, already keen to find their own voices, already questioning authority. The students I found at Wembley (as elsewhere) were highly motivated, competent individuals who simply needed the tools to transform their voices into confident, powerful, authoritative ones.

Chapter 4 provides space for the voices of Halifax bank managers, a selection from over the 300 that have completed the Advanced Diploma in Retail Banking Practice since the end of 2010. The Halifax is a company that is at the forefront of professional education in the UK with its innovative approach to management challenges by investing in its staff to enable them to think critically about current banking practice and to suggest ways the bank can improve.

Back in 2010 I was dispirited by the prescriptive nature of the course—looking at PEST, SWOT and reviewing high level skills, for example, seemed too narrow and constrained. I knew that the students needed to produce a viable business plan to improve branch performance, but I wanted the students to go further: I wanted them to discover a passion for learning. I suggested to them that broadening their reading would strengthen their educational experience and, to that end, I encouraged them to engage thoroughly with literature to substantiate their findings.

The Halifax is currently experiencing the effects of removing staff bonuses from their employee incentive schemes. A recent business plan made the compelling argument that removing bonuses deals only superficially with the question of how to improve the image of the organisation and that the root of the banking problem is sales culture: the manager and her staff need to foster a relationship founded on trust, empowerment and engagement. Using academic writers who comment more philosophically on business, such as John Hendry, students were able to find solid support for their contention regarding the importance of trust between all layers of employees and their argument that this trust was at the heart of sound management. All students had stories to tell about their branches, sometimes deeply unpleasant tales about abuse meted out to them by a public ignorant of the distinction between retail and investment banking as they wanted to direct their invective for the "banking crisis" at someone.

In my interviews with the Halifax students, I was struck by how they equated the interrogation of authority and the resisting of convention with real learning. In my role to provide clear and explicit direction on how to translate their ideas, experiences and research into resolving branch (and corporate) level problems, I encouraged them to engage with both fiction and non-fiction works in the form of Sillitoe's (1958) *Saturday Night, Sunday Morning* and Ferguson's (1998) *The House of Rothschild: Money's Prophets*. Students who read *Saturday Night, Sunday Morning* were able to comment on the relationship the characters have with money as well as the tensions between business and society. A student noted that the book's anti-hero, Arthur Seaton, has little respect for authority or business, and that business—in the shape of the factory where he and the other men in his community labour—"looms over the surrounding area". She concluded that the Halifax must not become an "overbearing" entity in the community and needed instead to position itself as a beacon of trustworthiness, friendliness and helpfulness within the community it served. Students who chose to read the historian Neill Ferguson's *The House of Rothschild* were able to draw valuable lessons from the brothers' closeness and unflagging cooperation and branch-level colleague engagement. Students used literature to examine the challenges faced by contemporary business in its quest to effect radical change in the banking culture: the collaboration between the Halifax and Middlesex University is no vacuous public relations exercise but a solid commitment to getting the best out of people.

Recently I have added another financial institution to the list of organisations with which I work, a group of American sales people pursuing an MA in coaching. Coaching is naturally susceptible to the cumulative triumphs of what I like to call "enriched training". There is an appeal to a reflective way of behavioural change, but ultimately as Drake (2007) argues, there is a deep need to work with stories in coaching, and a cumbersome reliance on behavioural orientation is simply not enough to help clients understand the connections between their identity and their stories. I have been impressed by Drake's research into using narrative coaching and intend to build on it by using literary characters' experiences in confronting the question of how to live so that, to paraphrase Thoreau, when we come to die, we discover that we had indeed really lived. My work with this new organisation and my incipient reflections on narrative coaching are beginning to emerge, and the question of narrative coaching is one that I intend to examine in subsequent research.

Chapter 5 details a less than satisfactory experience working with a group of young unemployed people selected by the Affinity Housing Group to work as apprentice chefs for Hüseyin Özer's Turkish restaurant group Sofra. Only one of the dozen or so students I had taught responded to my request for an interview. I thought the students had enjoyed our seminars together, but that enjoyment did not translate to submitting any written work. In a subsequent interview, the restaurant's proprietor suggested that that the problem with the course was that the students were not used to any actual work, academic or otherwise. Their previous experience of having little support with and not being particularly confident in school work necessitated some kind of preparatory time dedicated to communication skills, time management and work responsibility: this preparatory work, which might have served as a basis for academic and professional development, did not happen.

The student who responded to my request for an interview recalled the opportunity during the workshops to tell his story. Had I focussed on the students' stories and allowed the students to reveal themselves through narrative, had I trusted my instincts, I would have—maybe—helped the students to stay the course. I had never made the connection between Hüseyin Özer's love of telling his own fascinating story and the need the students had for telling their own. Each of the students I encountered at Sofra had his or her own story to reveal, a revelation of the self as well as a relational identity. Paul's memories of his recently deceased grandmother, "the only person who ever loved me and showed me that love through her cooking", Ginnifer's close relationship to her young daughter, Brian's casual yet painful references to being bullied, Lionel's distaste for educational recollections—I should have allowed all of their stories to unfold: all of their stories could have been used as a foundation for study and work. I had planned to use George Orwell's *Down and Out in Paris and London* to allow the students to enter imaginatively Orwell's experiences in difficult and even dangerous kitchens and to help the students find their own voices.

In Chap. 5, I also provide a discussion on Orwell's work as well as a study on the notion of "resilience", which is particularly relevant to the context of young people experiencing adversity and stress. In the end, the students felt as though they were perceived as incompetent and that their individuality was never recognised. I needed to have honoured each learner's history of experience, the stories of their ups and downs, details of familial and relationship challenges so that their wisdom could have emerged: the process of putting their stories into narrative form could have made the students' learning visible to them and I might have been able to report on a vastly different story.

My final chapter, Chap. 6, differs from the previous ones because it concerns individual students who are completing or have completed master's degrees or professional doctorates. These work based learning students who work full time are invariably at the top of their professions and are performing at a considerably advanced level at which I expect them to look at their work as critically as possible: they are expected to examine the relationships of power in the workplace and in society. What I hope the reader will discern in this chapter is the transformative impact reading literature has on the way these students conceptualise their working practice. The first part of the chapter is a discussion on how I encourage students to form a community of practice in order to increase their confidence. I then discuss how I started to think that if students seemed to understand their own work so much better by engaging with their fellow students' work, it would be profitable for them to look at novels that explore work, society, relationships and tensions within their own walks of life.

I chose Sinclair Lewis's (2006) *Babbitt* (a novel first published in 1922) for the coaching students primarily because of the eponymous character's search for his "true self". As coaches, the students are concerned with the obstacles preventing success in people's professional performances and George Babbitt's struggle to distance himself from the stultifying conformism and repressive materialism of early 20th century American middle class society seemed to offer a means of identifying common coaching themes and of facilitating clearer student writing.

It seemed a perfect fit to introduce students who were teachers and lecturers to John Williams' (2012) *Stoner*, a novel published in 1965 that tells the story of a college teacher in the Midwest between the two world wars. The students found immense value in reading *Stoner*: they purported to have understood human nature better through reading the story in the sense that their own teaching issues are so pellucidly illustrated in the novel.

A group of canine specialists reading Fred Gipson's (1956) classic *Old Yeller* or seafarers reading Richard Henry Dana's (1869) *Two Years Before the Mast* are exposed to a rich linguistic output that can enhance their critical analysis.

I have increasingly come to the realisation that my role is to instil a mode of trained literary discernment in my students, which can be delivered by having them read literary works and essays that demonstrate insight and clarity into the human condition. Ultimately, there is a preponderance of "learning models", expert business resources and books and journals on how practitioners can be more successful and their businesses can be more robust. We need to subject our idea of what a curriculum should look like to the most intense scrutiny. As students discover to their delight, and at times surprise, learning and literature not only complement each other, but can bring them closer towards wisdom.

Accepting the legitimacy of integrating literature into a work based learning curriculum is an urgent matter in higher education for the following reasons. Writing continues to be the dominant mode of communicating research and students need to learn how to write well. Students come from companies or their own businesses brimming with the will to succeed. They are generally experts in their fields and have little difficulty dealing with theoretical and evidence based research materials. We educators are able to demonstrate to them how to analyse text and to apply intellectually rigorous analysis of the materials with which they engage; we can also support them in addressing the complex and critical issues inherent in their disciplines or practices. It is the rare student, however, who fails to come unstuck when it comes to writing. The times I have heard "I know what to say, I just can't get it onto the page!" are too numerous to recount. Many of the academic writers I cite in the following chapters place considerable value on getting students to tell their stories. They put forward the hypothesis that storytelling draws us into each other's experiences, which has a transformative learning potential for us. As you will read, I believe that this perspective holds a great deal of weight: psychologists have long posited how the very act of constructing a story helps us to move towards a more integrated and unified way of learning (Mezirow 2000).

I have helped many frustrated writers by urging them to reframe their projects in terms of "telling a story". Elbow (1986) has a compelling theory that first-order thinking, the intuitive, creative free writing we do without direction or control should be followed by second-order thinking, logical, controlled, critical thinking, in order to foster better writing practices for students. His idea is that exploratory, free-writing on a subject followed by more critical writing becomes mutually reinforcing: "the fact remains that most people get more and better thinking—and less time wasting—if they start off generating" (p. 62). I coax first-order thinking by telling students to think of their first drafts as stories, stories which will help them to understand their experiences, position themselves in their narratives and allow them to write without the dreaded "block"—the obstacle of fear, of not being good enough, of not wanting to feel vulnerable and exposed.

I have found reminding students that even professional writers such as Hemingway typically discarded hundreds of drafts before a page emerged with which he was grudgingly content, or that Ralph Ellison first typed his drafts on typewriter and then tore them out to mark them up with pencil in a ruthless mania is integral to the process of supporting them to express themselves with less frustration and angst. Sometimes even showing them an excerpt from James Joyce who famously remarked "I can do anything with language I want" can help them address their expectations of creating perfect copy. There is no fool-proof recipe or fail-safe strategy to ensure clear, coherent and compelling prose. My fondest hope, though, is that these case studies I have presented in *Towards Wisdom* will encourage those involved in the nexus between education and business to develop an innovative and creative pedagogy for their students. Using stories in the shape of fiction, non-fiction, essays and poetry will help students to express themselves with more confidence and boldness.

I also believe that there is a pressing need to integrate literature into a work based learning curriculum, and, by extension, other business-based curricula. Works of literature, ordinarily confined to a humanities or literary course of study, help us to understand our experiences, our identities and our lives. As fewer students follow a course of study in the humanities, we have the perfect opportunity to introduce our students to stories of psychological dilemmas, loss, sadness, courage and spirituality composed with eloquence and insight into the human condition. Introducing more literary works offers students a more colourful and vivid palette to use when attempting to undergo the academic writing process, making such a process hopefully less of an endurance test and more of an exciting challenge. What I am endeavouring to create is a bond between the craft of the writer and the craft of the professional: it is self-evident that a merger can be effected between literature and professional studies.

I want to thank everyone who contributed to the making of *Improving Workplace Learning by Teaching Literature: Towards Wisdom*. Peter Critten, Neill Thew, Peter Swordy and Eva Brodin all read draft chapters and made perceptive and valuable comments that helped to bring shape and clarity to the work. Thank you also to Nick Calvert and Wendy Smith of the Halifax who provided extensive and helpful interviews and are incidentally a joy to work with. Thanks also to David Nicholson of the Halifax who agreed to write the preface. I further want to thank Mags Thomas for allowing me to interview her and her employees on site—their honesty and expansiveness are appreciated. Of course there are the students who allowed me to use their stories either in interviews or questionnaires. All are anonymised for the sake of consistency, even though most students didn't mind my identifying them personally. I appreciate the time and effort contributed by these storytellers who have been and continue to be inspiring. All have made this book what it is. The students from Toshiba, Wembley Stadium, the Halifax, the Sofra restaurant group and individuals from fields as disparate as canine training, health, coaching, education, maritime services, the police service, engineering and human resources have provided me with the most meaningful and interesting perspectives a researcher could ever wish for—thank you again!

References

Baldwin, J. (1984). *Notes of a native son*. Boston: Beacon Press.

Bruner, J. (2002). *Making stories: Law, literature, life*. Cambridge: Harvard University Press.

Dana, R. H. (1869). *Two years before the mast*. Boston: Fields & Osgood.

Drake, D. (2007). The art of thinking narratively: Implications for coaching psychology and practice. *Australian Psychologist, 42*(4), 283–94.

Elbow, P. (1986). *Embracing Contraries: explorations in learning and teaching*. New York and Oxford: Oxford University Press.

Ferguson, N. (1998) *The House of Rothschild. Money's Prophets 1798–1840*. London: Penguin Books.

Gipson, F. (1956). *Old Yeller*. Boston: Houghton Mifflin.

Lewis, S. (2006). *Babbitt*. London: Vintage Books.

Mezirow, J. (2000). *Learning as transformation: Critical perspectives on a theory in progress*. San Francisco: Jossey-Bass.

Sillitoe, A. (1958). *Saturday night, sunday morning*. London: Grafton Books.

Thoreau, H. D. (2007) *Walden* in Baym et al *The Norton Anthology of American Literature* Vol. B. New York: WW Norton & Co.

Williams, J. E. (2012). *Stoner*. London: Vintage Books.

Chapter 2
Opening up a World of Literature at Toshiba

The paradox of education is precisely this—that as one begins to become conscious, one begins to examine the society in which he is educated.

—James Baldwin

Abstract The happy, productive and healthy company is a corporate objective. Despite the misgivings expressed by some at Toshiba, on the whole employees seemed content and productive, yet there was a level of dissatisfaction with the then present practice. In this chapter I demonstrate how I used literature to help students learn more about work and themselves. I aim to reveal the relationship between learning and confidence and to explore how literature can support students in making a more substantial contribution to their organisations. If reflection is a fundamental requirement in high quality work, the capacity for reflection is nurtured by literature. The ability to deliver results, to possess commercial and business awareness, to work successfully in a team are all qualities encouraged throughout one's working life. My contention is that reflection on literature creates that breakthrough moment in students, that perception of themselves as confident professionals who can finally match their know-how to theory: students can use literature to become more reflective learners and employees. This chapter also describes how James Baldwin's "Notes of a Native Son" can be used to help students explore style and voice as well as socio-cultural issues such as racism and exclusion.

© The Author(s) 2016
C.A. Eastman, *Improving Workplace Learning by Teaching Literature*,
SpringerBriefs in Education, DOI 10.1007/978-3-319-29028-7_2

Introduction

In the spring of 2011 I began work with a half a dozen students from the Toshiba
Tec Corporation based at the company's UK headquarters in Chertsey, Surrey.[1]
These Toshiba employees were chosen to undertake the Certificate in Personal and
Professional Development because of their critical positions in Human Resources,
Operations, Marketing and Sales. They were to be "Ambassadors of Change",
charged with effecting a culture of transformation at Toshiba and had been selected
by the Head of Human Resources Mags Thomas to examine the challenges of staff
behaviour and performance. The aim of the certificate was to provide these key
people with the self-awareness and skills to enable them to drive change within their
own environments and for the organisation both within their own teams and across
the business. The desire for change, evidenced by the selection of these "ambassadors", strongly implies that there had been deep-rooted problems at Toshiba that
needed to be addressed, but from my own conversations with Mags and the students,
I discovered that these problems were no more serious than the day to day challenges
faced by any other organisation: "people don't say what they need to say"; "gossip
is rife here"; "there are definite communication issues". Granted, the issues that
Toshiba faced were of a particular complexion: communication, or lack thereof,
seemed to be the principal bone of contention at Toshiba, just in the same way as
other companies struggle with IT, aggressive management, unfair distribution of
workloads. There are as many petty problems as there are companies. If I may offer
a variation on an axiom formulated by Tolstoy in the opening of *Anna Karenina*: all
happy companies resemble one another; each unhappy company is unhappy in its
own way. The happy, productive and healthy company is a corporate objective.
Despite the misgivings expressed by some at Toshiba, on the whole, employees
seemed content, productive and healthy. But appearances count for little: as Paul
Gibbs (2013, p. 3) points out "the workplace is never homogeneous but messy,
complex and multilayered". Like Tolstoy's unhappy families, all is never quite what
it seems.

The desire for change at Toshiba emerged from a level of dissatisfaction with the
then present practice. Mags saw the work based learning curriculum as a means of
changing the culture at Toshiba. I saw the work based learning curriculum as a means
of introducing Toshiba students to the world of literature. What occurred in 2011
between the students and me has had significant consequences at Toshiba. The
company has now introduced the first industry Master's degree in sales appreciation
to help people learn the art of sales to a professional standard, and, in Mags' words
"an industry leading piece of work based learning is going on".[2] Toshiba is changing

---

[1]Toshiba Tec Corporation is a division of Toshiba that specialises in providing retail solutions,
principally photocopying and printing. In this Chap. 1 subsequently refer to this company simply
as Toshiba. The origins of the course and its structure will be delineated in the appendix, as will
any other relevant course or programme structures.
[2]Separate hour long interviews with Mags Thomas and the students were conducted a year after
not only the module but subsequent seminar discussions had finished.

for the better because "the quality of thinking" has improved skills and professionalism. Mags is in no doubt that "the performance of every individual who has been through [the certificate] has increased".

Drawing on essays examining the centrality of work to our identity as well as on Ron Barnett's work on will, Robert Coles' work on writing and voice and Elizabeth Anne Kinsella and Allan Pitmann's seminal work on phronêsis, I will demonstrate how I used literature to help students learn more about their work and themselves. I aim to reveal the relationship between learning and confidence and to explore how literature can support students in making a more substantial contribution to their organisations.

Background and Definitions

Before providing the background and context for my work with the Toshiba students, I would like to focus on definitions of terms that will be used in this chapter and in subsequent ones. As my claim is to improve workplace learning by teaching literature, it is imperative that I define precisely what I mean by "literature". According to the primary entry in the Oxford English Dictionary literature is defined as "written works, especially those regarded as having artistic merit; knowledge acquired from reading or studying books, especially the principal classical texts associated with human learning; literary culture, learning, scholarship". Further definitions include letters, books, printed matter of any kind (leaflets, brochures, advertisements) and written work valued for lasting artistic merit (OED 2012). The final definition—written work valued for lasting artistic merit—will be more applicable to the work I did with other cohorts, in particular, individual Masters and Professional Doctoral students.

With the Toshiba students I concentrated on articles from academic journals, particularly those on organisational change and books such as Peter Senge's *The Dance of Change* and Donald Schön's *The Reflective Practitioner*. The students were encouraged to explore the theories of John Dewey and Kurt Lewin, and all kept learning logs to record their observations and thoughts on their learning journeys.

Derek Attridge (2004, p. 13) broadly divides literature into two categories: the first, a more "literary" literature, distinguished by its complex handling of language and linguistic and stylistic aesthetics and the second, a more "instrumentalist" literature, in the light of a pre-existing set of assumptions, values, and goals that derive from the social and political realm". Although my focus with the Toshiba students was on the latter, the more "instrumentalist" type of literature, I believe that this kind of writing, although not literary in the sense outlined by Attridge, was effective in broadening their minds, challenging their ideological assumptions and alerting them to linguistic effects. Furthermore, at a time when "the crisis of the humanities" seems to be deepening, and there is urgency about "how we can talk about the value and the relevance of the humanities today" (Belfiore and Upchurch 2013, p. 6), I succeeded in exposing students to the meaning-making practices of human culture.

If the humanities are the "cultural bedrock of a democratic polity" (Small 2013, p. 126), I can claim that in my modest way I have helped to contribute to the health of democracy. We can discern in Mags' words the essence of a democratic organisation:

> Now, [after completing their academic work] all of them come to me with business wide concepts and ideas and programmes, whereas before, they tended to be very narrowly focussed. They encourage their colleagues to use the skill sets too of the learning disciplines they gained from doing their study. You can see that [knowledge] gets shared around.

The sharing of ideas, thinking broadly about the benefit of the organisation as a whole, collaborative working: all of these attributes appear to have been fostered by the work I did with these students. An emphasis on the humanities made them more attuned to each other's working practices. But how did this happen in practice?

When I was introduced to the programme of working with Toshiba, I concentrated on the freedom it afforded me rather than on the constraints it could have imposed.[3] It might be helpful if I summarise the programme agreement. The overview of the organisation's learning requirements stated that Toshiba "was looking for an alternative to staff development through appraisals as well as to introduce changes in staff behaviour and performance". This would be an undergraduate project module, which would be delivered over two university terms. The stated objective was to provide a group of "key people with the self-awareness and skills to enable them to drive change" across the business. The assessment strategies consisted of learning log extracts, a SWOT analysis[4] and a reflective essay. After meeting the students at Toshiba's offices in Chertsey and being impressed by their enthusiasm for learning and eagerness to explore their practice, I decided to focus intensely on the learning log aspect of the programme of study. The logs were divided into different sections under the following headings: date; noteworthy conversations, insights, reflections; an examination of conversations, meetings and ethical issues; and, most importantly, links to theories, reading, research, which could shed light on an event. For example, James observed tension between two key people in his department. To James, this tension appeared un-resolvable. In his final column he linked his observation with something applicable that he had read from Lewin: "Lewin (1951) views behaviour as a dynamic balance of forces working in opposing directions". I had encouraged the students to elaborate on as well as offer strategies, solutions and a rationale for their thinking.

Initially the students were expected to concentrate on workbook exercises. I designed and expanded the learning log to encourage their reading and research, to get them accustomed to exploring literature, which was and has always been my primary goal with work based learning students (see Eastman 2013, 2014). In order to illustrate this fully, I will provide information from an actual learning log. On 4 February 2011 Karl noted a conversation at a team meeting concerning the reporting

---

[3]The programme of activities for this group had been written before I started working for the Institute for Work Based Learning. I will refer to it in the appendix.
[4]SWOT is a structured planning method used to evaluate the strengths, weaknesses, opportunities and threats in a project.

of statistics. In "noteworthy conversations" he reported that Technician X was "very negative towards the stats, thinking that they were a 'waste of time'". In the "examination of conversations" column, Karl wrote that he explained to Technician X that his region had the best figures in the company and that he took time to explain to Technician X how the figures were produced, what they were based on and how beneficial they were. In his final column, linking his observations to his research, Karl was particularly expansive:

> Technician X is always very resistant to change and has complex needs which are probably never, ever going to be met by Toshiba. However, as Burnes (2009) suggests: people are emotional rather than economic-rational beings. I have explored his individual needs. As an employee, he does so much good work then destroys that work with one negative statement. His work is excellent but his attitude restricts his progress. I think that Technician X will eventually take note of the standards that are required. He has put himself into an awkward position and now must change permanently in order to achieve the levels of workmanship that Toshiba requires. As a manager I feel I have given him every opportunity to make these changes. He has been unfrozen – moved and re-frozen – in Lewin's words. My question is: will the fridge remain cold enough to keep Technician X where he is required to be?

With a touch of humour Karl reflects on his exchanges with Technician X. He justifies his behaviour using academic research and examines his duty as a manager with regard to managerial theories. This level of deep reflection is what Toshiba's "Ambassadors of Change" were aiming for. Change requires a profound understanding of one's current situation, and this is precisely what Karl was achieving in his learning log, grounding his empirical observations in the relevant theories he had come across in his research, which allowed him to illuminate his own conduct and that of others. A colleague of mine from the Institute for Work Based Learning at Middlesex expressed amazement at the work James, Karl and the others were producing. The assumption is that we should not expect such an in-depth engagement with literature from students who have had hitherto little to no experience of academic study. If we take as a given that the workplace is not organised as a place for learning, this level of reflection and engagement with literature is all the more extraordinary.

As Lum (2013, p. 31) points out in his relevant criticism of on-the-job learning provision, the fault lies with "the modern pre-occupation with 'learning outcomes', 'competences/skills' and all similar nomenclature associated with the bureaucratic compulsion to specify, measure and control". Not only must we never under-estimate our students' potential, we need to encourage them to develop their voices and to recognise the authority inherent in using their voices to articulate their distinctive positions in the workplace. Our goal as teachers is to get students to see that they have vested positions in an organisation, and their emerging voices can consolidate their authority as valuable members of that organisation.

Work, Identity and Reflection

The reflective aspect of work based learning has been comprehensively explored (Brookfield 1987; Dewey 2007; Kolb 1984; Schön 1991), so this is not the place to investigate the role of reflection in any great depth. However, it would be remiss of me not to discuss how the students used reflection in their practice. One of the students, Ian, puts it quite simply: "I reflect a bit more on situations now rather than just doing (a task) and moving onto the next one. I now think more about what went well or didn't go as well as I hoped and what I can do the next time." Ian's statement about reflection echoes the hundreds of statements about the importance of reflection that students have reported to me during the course of working with businesses. The idea of reflection definitely captures their interest, probably more than any other academic concept they examine. Winch (2013, p. 10) looks for a working definition of the workplace in the modern sense of earning a wage and decides that it is the site of an "agency" where "goods and services" are produced "with a view to remuneration". He concludes that the workplace is not "organised primarily for learning" (p. 11). This observation is important because it illuminates the reason why so many students find the secret to self-efficacy and confidence in reflecting on how and why they are able to manage an array of situations. Ian discussed his new way of working: "The way I work with the guys now is different. I think a bit more and I reflect on things. I now go back and think about how things could have been done better, whereas before I would have just moved onto the next task". Reflection appears to be a cornerstone of learning for students.

In his study of the transition of university graduates into full-time employment, Hinchcliffe (2013, p. 60) argues that the acquisition of skills, techniques and knowledge is simply not sufficient for individuals to manage their new occupation roles. Employers are looking for the ability to deliver results from graduates who can demonstrate the ability to intellectualise, think critically, problem solve creatively, communicate information clearly and be reflective. In fact, reflection is one of "the fundamental requirements" of employees, suggesting that the graduate "can operate well within a team and with clients, identify development and training needs and assess the efficacy of their own work".

Hinchcliffe is looking at the qualities valued in graduates and at employers' expectations of graduates. In work based learning programmes I have been working with people who, for the most part, have had little or no formal academic experience in higher education. Yet I find that these employees who have had little formal academic training share with university graduates a paucity of reflective skills. Reflection is not built into undergraduate degrees in the same way as it is a work based learning syllabus. Reflection is the cornerstone of what we practitioners of work based learning encourage in our students. Students that graduate from work based learning programmes appear to have the capacity for deep reflection that employers demand. If reflection is, as Hinchcliffe sustains, one of employers' "fundamental requirements" (2013, p. 60), work based learning offers the means to instil this quality in not only graduates entering the business, but also those already decades into the business. This capacity for reflection, I contend, is nurtured by literature. The ability to deliver results, to present ideas clearly, to possess commercial and business awareness, to work successfully in a team are all qualities recognised at the threshold of employment as well as throughout one's work life. For those employees who have not had the benefit of a formal academic education and presumably attendant exposure to critical thinking and formalised intellectual engagement, it is their reflection on literature that creates that breakthrough moment, that perception of themselves as confident professionals who can finally match their know-how to theory.

If we return to Karl's learning-log, we see how the marriage of know-how with the reflection on literature can work. Karl discusses a situation in which different departments do not appear to be committed to assisting each other:

> I was miffed that my region was short of technicians because several were doing work that should be covered by [another department]. Surely if they cannot cope, then we have a recruitment need. The situation that I found to have imposed on me as a manager has not been openly discussed at our various meetings. It has simply been assumed that if [this department] cannot cope then we will commit to helping them out. I think that with a more consultative approach all of our teams would be more committed to assisting each other by having a common goal.

Here is the workplace as a site of frustration that calls to mind Gibbs' (2013: 3) description of it as "messy, complex and multi-layered", which I quoted at the beginning of this chapter. Deranty (2008), a French psychoanalyst specialising in pathologies relating to work and the workplace, would state that Karl's situation is hardly abnormal: the nature and organisation of contemporary employment precludes co-operation and accentuates suffering. As Karl relates, the rules, regulations and technical procedures governing work processes resist the efforts of those who try to achieve productive ends. Dejours is pessimistic, claiming that lack of peer and self-approval can have a major pathological impact on one's life. Informed by his observations as a psychological consultant, he observes within a range of work places a problematic sense of identity caused by the perception of an uncertain future, a deterioration of working conditions and people afraid of losing their jobs, afraid of not being able to achieve targets, afraid of not being able to adapt to constant changes and afraid of the competition from peers both inside and outside the organisation. The individual becomes paralysed by anxiety and suffers angst and disappointment. Without the recognition of an individual's work, "the subject faces his or her own suffering, and it alone" (Deranty 2008, p. 37). Note that "recognition" is the crucial term. When Karl reflects on his practice by connecting theory to his observations, he discusses Senge's (1990) ideas on shared vision:

> A shared vision is a vision that many people are truly committed to because it reflects their own personal vision. If managed correctly, the whole [photocopier] installation problem could be solved simply by letting us as managers remove the obstacle that needs to be overcome. We would all then share the same vision which would be installations completed and satisfied customers.

When I interviewed Mags and asked her if the students' reading was good for business, she told me that they said that they had not realised that the material was out there, and did not realise that taking time to think through what they were doing would have such an impact on their practice. The students had started to adopt far more reflective attitudes toward their everyday decision making and had begun to observe a "richness" of thinking and doing because of having reflected on tasks. She said that this new, fresh way of thinking was observable in a colleague who had been part of the course:

> I see it in Emily. Whereas before she might have had a tendency to have a go at something, immediately when she started the course, she was coming back to me and telling me about her thinking and what has taken her there and how her thinking has given her a range of options. She might say that she has gone for this specific option but has realised the potential of the others as well. There is a richness to her thinking about even the smallest of things.

Ben pointed out how important it was to be upfront and honest with people even though there could be a bad reaction to the information "you needed to convey". He used Burnes' (2009) article on ethics and organisational change to make the point that no matter how difficult the day-to-day pressures to meet deadlines and performance targets were, it was important to act ethically at all times. The students' recognition that not only what they were doing was valuable, but also that their frustrations, irritations, hunches, experiences and perceptions were reinforced by their reading was instrumental in their learning. This epistemic acknowledgement, to borrow Dejours' formulation (Deranty 2008), is the only way work becomes a meaningful experience, strengthening one's identity by engaging one's intelligence.

Raelin (2007, p. 77) sees this recognition manifesting itself in "team-work sensitivity", "managing politics", "handling pressure": identity is crucial because "learning who one is, through the doing of work, is inevitable". So how does reflecting on literature strengthen one's identity? Hinchcliffe (2013, p. 53) makes the perfectly valid observation that identity—workplace or otherwise—as a concept—"runs into the sand the moment it is grasped". There are many workplace identities. However, if, as he suggests, we concentrate on the "structural features" of workplace identity, we can make meaningful points. These structural features comprise values, intellect, performance and engagement, as suggested by his research project into what employers were looking for in graduates. As Hinchcliffe reminds us, the world of work is hardly a "value-free, technocratic domain" (p. 58). People need to demonstrate that they can be trusted: their personal ethics are transparent in their social dealings at work.

The research and reading the students undertook could be perceived as demanding in the context of full time employment. Work based learning students have to find time outside of work hours to read, research and write, but most find the research and reading extremely fulfilling because, sometimes for the first time, their own observations and ideas are substantiated in print by academics, practitioners and industry experts. As Emily observes:

> Reading the different literature really opened my eyes to see different sides of things and to see how people think in different areas. Reading helps us to see a range of scenarios. In just

thinking differently and being open, you are able to reflect on new ways of thinking about things and [are thus able to have] more of a positive impact.

Shared values, as the students have brought up on more than one occasion, are central to a team. Reading and reflecting on Burnes' article which advocates a return to the ethically based approach to change promoted originally by Kurt Lewin became a central and compelling feature in the students' thinking and writing. Through reading Burnes' article, the students learned that one of Lewin's central preoccupations was the importance of democratic values and how to spread these values throughout society. Lewin had conducted research with seminal results into the effects of both autocratic and democratic atmospheres on people; and, in one of his studies on groups of children, he concluded that in an atmosphere in which children could make their own decisions democratically, they fought less and were friendlier towards each other. His pioneering work became the core of *Organization Development,* which looked at how organisations and individuals could function better. An important aspect of functioning within a democratic society and a democratic organisation was recognising and combating racism, discrimination and prejudice.

I asked students to examine their own backgrounds and to reflect on whether their interests and beliefs originated in their background. Although this chapter is concerned less with the exploration of more literary literature such as essays and novels (which I shall explain in depth in other chapters) and more with the academic literature I suggested the Toshiba students explore, Barbara used some of this more "literary" literature in her reflections on her practice. In particular she studied James Baldwin's essay "Notes of a Native Son" (1955) (from *Notes of a Native Son*) in order to examine Baldwin's style and use of voice. She comments on Baldwin's passion, conviction and honesty and perceives the racism that blighted his life:

> I felt longing for the writer, longing for him to be able to go back to the time when he realised his father had shared some kindnesses with him many years ago. But due to the self-loathing that his father had, this had prevented him from exuding any warmth or crumb of comfort to this family for so long that [hostility and unhappiness] had become a way of life to them all. He talks of the year he had contracted some dreadful, chronic disease of fever and fire in the bowels and at first I thought he was referring to the daily racism which he and everyone around him were subjected to – racism, which would be tantamount to a disease.

As Barbara's narrative illustrates, the literary text can be interpreted in a socio-cultural way. She does not simply imagine the tensions of difference from Baldwin's account, she faces the racial issues head-on. West (1996, p. 144) writes persuasively about the need for teachers to urge their students to engage with conflict. We need to use conflict as a "heuristic", to try to get students to reflect on "how to live", how to make meaning, how to recognise the "inexhaustibility of difference". Baldwin's powerful testimony of racism is far stronger than any kind of "recognising diversity" training course.

Similarly, Hinchcliffe's structural features of intellect, performance and engagement can be broadened and enhanced by a wide engagement with literature. Through literature, students can reflect on and examine their social values—cultural and diversity awareness—values which were strongly endorsed by employers in

Hinchcliffe's study. We see that looking at others' stories helps us to reflect on our own values. But for students to tell their own stories, they need to find their own voices.

Voice

I have been running workshops on voice not only for Masters Degree students and Professional Doctoral candidates but also for new researchers at Middlesex University for the past two years. From a range of topics I examined—avoiding clichés, how to reinforce an argument, how to analyse texts, how to self-edit—I began to focus primarily on voice. I framed this topic by emphasising how each of us has a story to tell, a story that allows us to qualify and interpret what we observe and read. Students looked at how points of view are handled, how pieces of writing are organised, which metaphors and images writers employ and what evidence they use to support their conclusions. I will be discussing the work I do with individual Masters Degree and Doctoral candidates in detail in the final chapter. My interest in exploring voice and recognising its importance in helping students express themselves, however, emerged from my work with the Toshiba students. I was impressed by the students' collective enthusiasm for and pride in their work, but I realised that if they were unable to develop strong, confident voices, they would not be able to articulate their stories.

Barnett (2004, p. 90) provides an illuminating discussion of voice that has informed my own perceptions. He points out that voice is much more than mere utterances but "a projection of the self". As he expands his argument, he states that there are two voices—the embodied and the metaphorical. The former is the vocalising of our thoughts and feelings; the latter is the authentic placing of oneself in the world—what many academics call "positionality". The embodied voice is the voice that is present or absent—it is when the student makes a classroom contribution, for example. The metaphorical voice may take some time to come into its own—it is when the student becomes "authentic" (p. 92). The embodied voice may not necessarily be authentic. If a student is simply echoing without reflection what she has read, the metaphorical or authentic voice is absent. Therefore, it is this metaphorical or authentic voice that we want to encourage. Barnett's point is that the students who put themselves forward by expressing themselves, by overtly performing, may not be authentically communicating: there are many reasons the authentic voice may be suppressed. I will be drawing on what writers such as Barnett and others perceive as obstacles to thwarting the authentic voice and then detail how I addressed each obstacle in my work with the Toshiba students.

> I feel that I was taken on a journey, that there was a lot of trust and that you could pretty much study what you wanted to study. I realised I had a voice when people gave me feedback. It encouraged me to go forward and do more work and read more. We spoke extensively on

what we read. It opened a whole new world of writers and thinking I didn't know existed and made me feel more confident.

This is Karl revealing how essential it is to feel safe enough to develop an authentic voice. Higher education can suppress voice. Elbow (2007) notes that students have been discouraged from including their own feelings and stories in academic discourse. To participate in anything, let alone in higher education, we need to speak in our own voice. Speaking in neutral tones—perhaps those occurring by emulating other more authoritative voices—does not allow students to use language inflected with their own identity. West (1996) argues that higher education discourages conflict, tension and dissensus: students are afraid to vent their true feelings because there is not enough reflective engagement with the tensions and differences in society. Barnett (2004, p. 95) reminds us that the simple instruction "tell me more" to students can neutralise their fears, make students bolder in amplifying their thoughts as well as invite them to "disclose their being".

In my first Chertsey session with the Toshiba students, I could sense their anxiety. They did not know what to expect and were worried about what they had "got themselves into". I have subsequently heard that statement, more or less phrased that way, from hundreds of students over the years. Higher education may suppress the voice and undergraduates may find themselves in a perpetual struggle with essay deadlines, referencing guidelines and a vast array of pedagogical novelties such as lecture note-taking, drafting literature reviews and developing the ability to write differently to meet different expectations. The Toshiba students and the other students I will be discussing had not had the luxury of acclimatising themselves into the higher education milieu. More often than not, they were forced to come to terms with referencing conventions, how to read with purpose and how to write clearly about their practice right from the outset. Making students feel safe is critical, and this feeling of safety can be engendered by the "tell me more" philosophy Barnett advocates. "Tell me more" invites an authentic voice which can then be harnessed to a story.

In order to block out the multiple voices students are subjected to in higher education, they must be encouraged to find out how they really feel and how others really feel. One of the first things I tell students regarding their reading and research is that not all writing is equal: there are many articles and books replete with obfuscatory, opaque and downright ambiguous language. I advise them to find something on the same subject by a different writer, a writer with more accessible prose. Students will quickly discover that a great deal of writing is from an objective stance, and, although some disciplines lend themselves to more informational and objective and less narrative and persuasive language, students learn to produce prose that has a voice and sounds like a person (Elbow 2007). Speigelman (2001) makes the perceptive point that we do not even note stories that have been woven seamlessly into the most successful arguments: the personal story helps the argument flow, and we are then persuaded by the writer.

The beauty of a work based learning curriculum is its flexibility and its propensity to extract relevant material form a range of disciplines. I encouraged the Toshiba students to read excerpts from Peter Senge's *The Dance of Change*, (arguably from a social science/business discipline). They read excerpts from John Dewey's *How We Think* (sociology/philosophy), Kurt Lewin's *A Dynamic Theory of Personality* (psychology) and they dipped into journals from social sciences, physical sciences and the arts and humanities. Students were especially impressed by the *Dance of Change* because of the story format. Speigelman's (2001, p. 64) argument that stories can serve the same purposes as academic writing and that "narratives of personal experience can accomplish seriously scholarly work" appears prima facie as uncomfortably radical, but I do not think we can ever over-emphasise the power of personal insight. If we return to Barbara's comments on Baldwin's "Notes of a Native Son", we can see Speigelman's point illustrated clearly:

> I thought [this essay] thought provoking and immensely powerful, written with passion and conviction. I found it sad and his honesty repulsed me at times. I felt longing for the writer to go back to a time when he realised that his father had shared some kindnesses with him many years ago. I was frustrated that due to the self-loathing that he and his father had, there was no warmth or crumb of comfort in the family for so long that [bitterness] had become a way of life to them all.

Barbara has picked up on the poison of racism and the excoriating effect living as a second class citizen had for the narrator. She has responded to Baldwin's unique voice, which is not confessional or therapeutic but instead is fashioned into an argument in which personal experience is used evidentially to illustrate a specific position. It did not take the Toshiba students long to recognise that the voice is the writer's persona, the writer's authority, the writer's positionality. Danielwicz (2008, p. 420) states that, although it seems "counter-intuitive", good writing should eschew public topics and focus on the "personal". Her contention is that when students write impersonally, they have a difficult time making cognitive connections: the "I" should be at the centre of a student's writing to develop their voice and authority. She enlarges her discussion by emphasising the political nature of voice: "a public voice results from the writer's engagement and position in the world. Our texts are powerful only in relation to other readers and texts" (423). It is critical to bring to the workshop or seminar the at times unacknowledged fact that voice can be a catalyst for political debate. For work based learning students, and indeed many other students, academic writing can appear an amorphous mass of words on different subjects: teams, change, resources, productivity, profitability, values. When students begin to discern the political and power implications—the distinctive positions writers construct for themselves by using their voices authoritatively—students gain insight into how voice functions.

In an early discussion about "silo" mentality at Toshiba, James brought up the fact that there appeared to be some degree of envy directed at the students chosen to do the Middlesex University course.[5] He said that the perception was that "all this learning stuff was a waste of time and that their jobs were about customer care—doing it, not learning about it". The students discussed this and subsequently wrote

---

[5]The expression "silo" originates from the late 1980s idea that a "silo" system is one incapable of reciprocal operations with other systems and suggests a rigid and controlling mind set.

about it, recognising that underlying this accusation was the fear and anxiety that power dynamics at the company were changing. Perhaps there was "something in this learning" that would privilege those involved and exclude others to the extent that those not involved in "all this learning stuff" would have their jobs threatened? Group psychology is beyond the purview of my discussion here, but I want to illustrate how emotive a subject learning or education is. There is a school of thought that promotes the idea that voice is antithetical to team working and that human development and learning is about community and "communities of learning" (Lave and Wenger 1991). Students recognised the value in team work, in mutual respect, in getting along. As Mags pointed out, the students continued to share their learning even after the course had finished:

> You regularly see them now as the ones who encourage their colleagues and *challenge* their colleagues and introduce their colleagues to the skills set of the learning discipline that they gained from doing their study. You can see that this learning gets exponentially shared around and gets mirrored by their colleagues in terms of doing things.

I would argue that this "challenging" (in Mags' words), in particular, comes from the students having developed their own voices. Before they even start their course, they recognise the influence a powerful voice can have. They have probably even been persuaded by an argument that had a compelling story interwoven within its text. They had encountered authoritative writing, yet they were most likely not part of these public narratives. Through examining powerful voices in literature and allowing their own emerging voices to result from these explorations, students gain in confidence and recognise that the personal is invariably political. Barbara saw that what she was learning had implications for her entire team:

> It is important to have the authority to get on with it, to be trusted to come up with our own views where someone is not going to bang you down or chop you down in two seconds flat. That's fantastic. [Reading Baldwin] made me think about my own staff. Am I cutting them short or not letting them flourish?

These activities such as reading, reflecting, soul-searching and transformation take a great deal of will. As Barnett (2004) demonstrates, learning is ideally a two-way relationship. It is important for a teacher to be inspiring, for example, in suggesting interesting literature to explore. Inspiring learning can be described. Ian attends to the difference between what he has perceived as "training" and what he has now experienced as inspirational learning:

> The difference between corporate training and *real* education – what we have here – is that with corporate training, people come in, give you a massive folder of stuff and expect you to work through it. It doesn't mean anything to me. Whereas with this University course, you get a few pages, read them in depth and then reflect on them. There's more essence; there's more to it than a training course.

Ian is describing the concept of "knowledge ownership". The training company, presumably briefed by the organisation, imposes its ideas on what employees need in order to improve their practice. As Lewis (2013, p. 33) emphasises, because there is an assumption that workplace knowledge is the property of the employer, the workers feel that their knowledge is valuable and "may resist attempts to appropriate the knowledge upon which they draw to perform work if they believe that sharing could devalue their unique work to the organization, making them more expendable". What more enlightened organisations have realised is that practitioners have the most knowledge about what they do. They are more than capable of finding creative solutions to problems. The challenge is, as Lewis sees it, is that most of this knowledge remains "inarticulate and latent" (p. 35).

A training company coming in with its own ideas about how to increase productivity or how to create real leadership potential and its "massive folder of stuff" is incapable of tapping into the knowledge and insights of the field practitioners—people who are doing the job every day. This is because the wealth of organisational knowledge, including tacit knowledge, resides in the insights of the employees. When the employees are encouraged to articulate their knowledge, own their knowledge, and make their knowledge explicit, they are then able to make these insights available to the company for which they work. In Lewis' words: "Ownership perceptions are the key to sharing" (p. 35). Ian suggests that favourable organisational contexts need to be created for that to happen: employee education rather than employee training is the way that an organisation can demonstrate it is relinquishing its desire to control knowledge and recognising instead that the knowledge of its people is where the real wealth resides.

Mags discusses the next step for the Toshiba students:

> My view is now that what the students really need is to get themselves into a strategic project to look at the complete wider business because it is very silo-like as many businesses are. So to me there is a piece of work around organisational design, being really quite radical by getting the guys to look at whether the design of an organisation is now fit for purpose. What they are all telling me is that the organisation design here has now outgrown what is appropriate and fit for the business, so to me that would be a good project: looking at an entire business as to whether it is fit for the future because I don't believe that this business is. Something could be done by having their ideas and input.

Training providers are interested in grafting their own ideas and input onto employees' current knowledge. Work based learning looks to best practice solutions within the students. Predicated on unearthing best practice solutions is pedagogical guidance or, as Barnett (2004, p. 117) would have it, "inspirational teaching". For that group of wary students I encountered back at the beginning of 2011 in their Chertsey boardroom office, I had to think about how I could inspire them:

> Inspirational teaching requires that the teacher be himself inspired in some way. There has to be a passing on of spirit or, rather, the teacher's spirit comes to be taken up in the student. The taking-up is only partly metaphorical. The spirit evident in the teacher's *enthusiasm*, finds an echo in the student. The echo is not the original sound, but a further rendition of it. However, the student then infuses this spirit with her spirit: she fans its flames. She warms it and is warmed by it. She may even glow with excitement, seeing her curricula and pedagogical experiences in a new way (Barnett 2004, p. 117).

Barnett admits that this description of "inspiring" could be rightly perceived as puzzling and elusive. It certainly eschews any rules, techniques or systems. Like Barnett, I don't believe that there is a template that can be rigorously adhered to.

Within the spirit of work based learning—learning about how to "move around" the workplace and how to reach the limits of one's "mastery, expertise or, indeed, phronêsis (practical wisdom)" is paramount (Gibbs 2011, p. 21). When I considered some of the materials suggested to me to use with the new Toshiba cohort—a workbook with tasks including engagement statements and SWOT and PEST analyses – I was uninspired. I needed to think of far more stimulating and creative ways to address the learning outcomes of the module. I have always been convinced of the need to articulate one's thoughts and ideas as articulately as possible so I decided to concentrate on writing as a vehicle for the students to demonstrate their knowledge. Given that the written word is the dominant mode of communication in all university subjects and the Toshiba students, were, after all, on a university course, writing became my principal area of concern.

In an article examining market orientation demands in higher education, Molesworth et al. (2009, p. xvi) make the semantic point that students need to think of themselves as learners rather than people aiming to possess a degree. Possessing impoverishes the learning experience: "a desire to *have* reduces the individual's experience to desire, for something external—a commodity. In doing so, self-knowledge and a satisfaction in one's practice is disallowed". I remain unconvinced that self-knowledge and a satisfaction in one's own practice can be compromised or tarnished by the desire for a material acknowledgment. In my experience, graduation and the receiving of a certificate, diploma or degree are the objectives when the student studies hard. The will to succeed is motivated by the end-goal of graduation. I recognise that the authors are referring to traditional, in the main, young undergraduates and that our more mature practitioners will be naturally imbued with different concerns. I further recognise that the authors' emphasis is on the pedagogical constraints wrought by marketisation in higher education. However, a student's ability to enter into academic conversations is less inhibited by marketisation and more promoted by inspirational teaching—teaching that helps the student realise her own authentic self-creativity. What is required is "a continuing and patient effort to so configure the total pedagogical environment, such that students come into spaces of their own" (Barnett 2004, p. 125). I interpret Barnett's exhortation by encouraging students to devour literature that will increase their self-knowledge.

As part of the learning outcomes for the course, the students had to write a development plan. Barbara wanted to investigate stress as a major contributory factor to absence in the workplace. She read thoroughly from research in occupational health as well as from a series in the *Harvard Business Review* on stress related problems within the workplace. From the outset of our sessions together, I encouraged the students to read widely and pointed out that the *Harvard Business Review* contained many articles by practitioners, a fact which at times made their reading more relevant and certainly more accessible. Many articles in the *Review* read like stories as well. I thought it was prudent to direct the students to more conversational articles while they were developing their own voices because the voice of a more "academic" article could alter or even warp their own tentative voices before they even started. Nesi (2012, p. 61) suggests that students try to imitate without fully comprehending the impersonal and "densely informative texts" they are presented with. The results are understandably badly digested, inchoate, even incomprehensible texts. She has found that even at post-graduate levels, students' academic writing is deficient: "It seems sensible to assume that most students will be familiar with informal, interactive, implicit language features" (p. 61).

These are the language features most prevalent in conversation and fiction. Of course it is unavoidable that there are set texts and specific "densely informative texts" within certain disciplines. The work based learning curriculum has the freedom and flexibility to allow students to pursue "evidence" in the shape of academic work that can be more accessible like the articles in the *Harvard Business Review* and, of course, stories and fiction. Barbara wrote that she thought there were some managers at Toshiba who have "kept quiet" because they were too busy or because of their "inherent desire to be liked": she reinforces her observation from her *Harvard Business Review* article which stated that if managers' work groups still show suboptimal performance after the familiar tool kit of interventions, the manager should be replaced.

Barbara's mordant point that certain staff are "allowed" to carry on working at a high level of poor performance leads into a narrative about how she then approached the HR Manager with her ideas about forming a well-being group to combat stress and to see what could be done about what she perceived as a "serious" issue that could be "systematically addressed". When she read the Baldwin essay she was able to link the narrator's feelings of "not being heard" in a Black ghetto in the United States in the 1950s to what was happening in some pockets of her organisation. She was able not only to draw parallels between Baldwin's fictionalised study and what she perceived was happening to some employees, she used Baldwin's powerful dissection of the anomie, apathy and simmering resentment in the ghetto to highlight potential problem areas within her company:

> We have approximately 270 employees in our company. In our financial year we lost 1308 days to sickness absence. We have had untold disciplinary, grievance, capability and attendance management meetings resulting in 207 working days on performance management alone.

Barbara does not simply detail grievance after grievance duly reinforced with appropriate academic research. She is capable of coming up with potential solutions:

> We do so many things right at our company and that's why I'm here, but we need to get a handle on absences and stress.

She suggests sending out a staff survey to gauge feedback as well as giving details to all staff about healthy eating and organising a lunch-time exercise group. Barbara had the will to research this topic thoroughly. When a student embarks on a major personal project of her own, her "will" becomes a "constituent" of her own identity (Barnett 2004, p. 20). Barnett believes that a student's will must be engaged in order for the student to be committed to her learning: "without the will, nothing will be learnt by the student and no claim will be made by that student that can bear any weight" (26). To my mind, the will to learn needs to be captured then in a receptacle the student can use with the least amount of frustration. Attridge's (2004) claim that literature need not apply only to the production of high or elite culture—that "literature" can be applied to a range of inventive literatures is a useful reminder here.

The Value of the Humanities

Robert Coles, the Pulitzer Prize winning child psychiatrist and Harvard professor of social sciences, introduced reading literature (novels, poetry, short stories) into the Harvard graduate curriculum in the fields of medicine, law, education and business. In an interview published in the *Journal of Education*, he explained the difference between how he taught literature at the Harvard graduate schools and how it has been conventionally taught (since the 1970s):

> I don't teach [literature] the way many English professors teach. They teach deconstructionism, which actually is a version of, a reductionist version of, of psychoanalysis, and stay clear of moral issues. They are really a parody of what some psychoanalysts are – just cleverness, which is a curse to the students. Some English teachers are into those French theorists who so often stand for nothing, who are basically nihilists. I'm appalled! Thank God, I still love to read for the stake of reading from stories – something that may connect with how I live my life. (Ryan and Jenkins 1997, p. 2).

Coles' words capture what I am endeavouring to do within a work based leaning curriculum—to introduce the humanities, the branch of learning concerning human culture, particularly fields that contain the study of "arts, letters and morals" (Belfiore and Upchurch 2013, p. 1)—to working practitioners who can use the study to address the challenges of their own working lives. I wanted to do this because my own background as an English teacher could enable me to introduce students to literary culture as well as enable them to use the textual power of well crafted literature to write clearly. When I was introduced to the syllabus intended for the Toshiba students I thought that too much of it was task-focused and seemed to concentrate on skills acquisition at the expense of effecting a real educative transformation, hence my turning to literature.

PEST and SWOT analyses, as useful as they are for providing a stimulus for discussion and an aperçu into an organisation's performance, need to be aligned to a far more robust way of getting students to think about themselves, to attend to how others think and to be responsive to a world of possibilities. Arguably employers want their employees to think broadly and to be capable of reflection. Emphasising the point that a task-based work based learning curriculum could be perceived as narrow, Hinchcliffe (2013, p. 64) advocates harnessing "the humanities" (what he terms as the "traditional staple of liberal education programmes") to expand the horizons of work based learning students. For example, when addressing the challenges of organisational change, he suggests what the enthusiasts of "learning through doing" could consider is having students read Giusseppi Tomasi di Lampedusa's *The Leopard*, which although set in 1860s Sicily and concerned with the political, social and amorous travails of a superannuated aristocrat, would be far more "enjoyable" and "instructive" for students to read than any number of books detailing the theories of change management (p. 65).

Except for Baldwin's "Notes of a Native Son", the students were not introduced to any "literary" texts; however, using the articles I have already detailed made me audacious enough to integrate more literary reading, such as Sinclair Lewis's *Babbitt*, novels from Richard Henry Dana, John Williams, Alan Sillitoe, Fred Gipson and excerpts from 18th, 19th and 20th century essayists with cohorts from Wembley Stadium, the Halifax and both Masters and Doctoral students (discussions in subsequent chapters). My thinking behind proposing this book *Improving Workplace Learning by Teaching Literature* originated in a remark made by a colleague when I was delivering a survey of 19th century American literature that included Herman Melville's *Moby Dick*. He remarked pessimistically that he doubted that 50 years hence would see *Moby Dick* or indeed any of Melville's oeuvre being included on any literature syllabus except perhaps in an abridged format. Moreover, he despaired for the future of the humanities in general—as tuition fees increased, returns for students studying the humanities would simply not be great enough to secure their survival.

Belfiore and Upchurch (2013, p. 35) have edited a series of essays that examine the state of the humanities. The authors detail the history of their specific disciplines in the Academy and offer debates on their "utility" in an atmosphere dictated by inescapable economic considerations. They trace two discourses relevant to the discussion on the decline of the humanities—the rhetoric of "doom and gloom" in which the humanities are increasingly marginalised within a university system that has adopted a "business-like approach" to its curricula and perceive the humanities as "useless"; those who promote the humanities as having "an important contribution to make to boosting the national economy, to social cohesion, to individual quality of life".

The skills of rhetoric, of composing persuasive texts, of "deriving interpretative narratives" (Parker 2013, pp. 51–52) are enshrined in the humanities, and, in particular, the teaching of literature. In one of the essays "The Futility of the Humanities", Michael Bérubé describes his experiences teaching "general education" in the humanities at Pennsylvania State University to students in engineering, law, nursing, kinesiology, making the observation that the more "remote" the students' majors were from the humanities, the weaker their reading and writing skills tended to be:

> We will find that when student reading and writing is the measure of academic achievement, the disciplines that are founded on practices of reading and writing will suddenly appear central to the educational mission of the university (Bérubé 2013, p. 75).

Phronêsis or Practical Wisdom

As the subtitle of this book is *Towards Wisdom*, it may be useful to explain the connection between teaching literature and wisdom. Kemmis (2012: 148) points out that since the aim of professional education is to develop professional knowledge in a broad sense, we should be encouraging craft knowledge and personal knowledge, not only on an individual basis but also within a community of practice. He makes the intriguing observation that we should think of phronêsis as "professional practice plus". We want good practitioners, we want wise practitioners, but phronêsis is not something that can be taught—it can be learned only by experience. For Kemmis the "plus" is the "something a bit more" than knowledge: it is desiring someone to act ethically. For example, on a day to day basis, practitioners have to find the best ways to deal with situations. A manager realises that he has to deal with a member of his team. He will have to determine a diagnosis to suit these particular circumstances—a close knit team, a member of which is negative and hyper-critical of others, customer considerations. Practice, skill and judgment are all called for in these circumstances. The good, sound judgement is the "plus": my contention is the "plus" is immeasurably enhanced by the reading of literature.

Here is Karl exploring the challenges of dealing with a colleague on the team who is resistant to change:

> I am questioning myself. Is there a need to change X? What would it achieve in the long run? After all, his work is excellent and it is just his negative attitude that is draining me and the rest of the team. For example, he is constantly complaining that the equipment we supply is not what he would have chosen. Even though X's work is, as stated, excellent, I think that he needs to be more positive. If he did become more positive, the effect on the team as a whole would be better in terms of team spirit which can affect output, customer relations and morale in general. He is a respected member of my team, so I need to think about how to change his attitude.

Karl is faced with a difficult decision that necessitates his acting wisely. What happens is that Karl uses Burnes (2009) to reflect on how to deal with the team member whose negativity threatens the rest of the team and, by extension, the company. Karl explains that something is needed beyond a pragmatic approach: he knew he needed to address the negative team member's emotions. He appealed to him, therefore, on an emotional level, stressing how badly affected the whole team had been by his unhelpful attitude, persuading him emotionally to take responsibility for his actions. The ethical literature Karl uses to inform his considered and wise approach must be highlighted.

Marker (2013, p. 11) reminds us that when organisational leaders make unwise decisions, "their organisations suffer, and so can society". Wisdom is not rooted in any scientific knowledge—it is both a cultural and metaphysical concept, something Sternberg (2003, p. 152) defines as "the application of successful intelligence and creativity as mediated by values toward the achievement of a common good." Karl wants to act wisely and I would suggest that foremost in his mind is the long-term health and survival of his team, and, by extension, Toshiba as a company. He shrewdly discerns the problems negativity can produce even for a "respected member of a team" who continues to perform "excellent" work.

There is a growing body of scientific evidence that demonstrates that emotions not only affect our perceptions but "at the level of neurological circuitry", they appear to be "deeply embedded in the machinery of thought" (Hall 2010, p. 65). Karl is not a neurologist—he has instead used years of accumulated experience and wisdom to recognise the potential problems negative emotions can have on an individual and on those with whom the individual works. This practical wisdom or phronêsis emerges from Aristotleian philosophy, for, as Aristotle (2009, p. 115) observed: "the work of man is achieved only in accordance with practical wisdom as well as with moral virtue". Kinsella and Pitman (2012, p. 4) translate Aristotle's ancient concept of phronêsis for a modern readership who wish to see how it can be usefully employed in considering professional knowledge. They note that phronêsis implies reflection and examine what it might "look like" in professional practice.

Karl was able to embrace uncertainty and go beyond competence. He was taking a risk by directly confronting the negative employee and explaining the ethical implications of his behaviour. Because the processes of most professions are limited by outcome based needs, people can be dissuaded from using their own creative and wise initiatives to resolve problems: there is inevitable a manual, a set of guidelines, an HR directive which will demonstrate what you are supposed to do in the event of any situation. Karl's and others' work demonstrate emphatically the integration of sound knowledge enhanced by literature into one's own experienced practice can result in deep meaning for our students. It is therefore important that we develop teaching practices in which not only the students' wisdom is encouraged to flourish but the wisdom derived from literature frames the educational discourse.

In an essay that attempts to recover Aristotle's concept for the professionals, Ellnett Jr (2012, p. 15) states that phronêsis need not be restricted to the "range and scope of professional judgments". He asserts that "one can be a good professional and also be a good spouse, a good parent, a good promoter of world-class university rowing" but being a professional "is a very important part of living a good life" (14). Karl's concerns about his negative colleague evince a keen sense of professional identity and, the ultimate marker of a professional, a resourceful and ever-present need to "respond to changing conditions, resources and problems" and to exercise practices that "absorb new knowledge and ways of working" (Edwards 2010, p. 5). Karl is able to integrate literature on change to amplify and enrich his (wise) observations:

> For Lewin (1935) change was less about achieving a particular objective and more about individuals and groups learning about themselves. He claimed that in doing so, these individuals and groups would of their own volition be prepared to change their behaviour. I need to find a way of exposing X to his own negativity in order to start his learning process. A change in our working practices must come from the people above us. Burnes (2009) notes that an organisation's ethics are embedded in its culture. Consequently, attempting to change the norms of behaviour in an organisation by adopting an ethical code, for example, is over optimistic. We, the everyday practitioners and managers can effect positive change by modifying our own behaviours.

When students engage with literature, their observations are deepened and their sense of social and professional bonds is heightened.

Russell (1996, p. 9) reflects: "Social cohesion is a necessity, and mankind has never succeeded in enforcing cohesion by merely rational arguments". All of the Toshiba students' concerns centred on social cohesion in the workplace. My contention is that the humanities not only foster independent intelligence and critical thinking skills, they are also "the cultural bedrock of a democratic polity" (Small 2013, p.126) according to those who argue for their relevance, profitability and power. One of the most high profile, recent writers who equate the humanities with a healthy, functioning democracy is Martha Nussbaum (2010, p. 21):

> If this trend [of marginalising the humanities] continues, nations all over the world will soon be producing generations of useful machines, rather than complete citizens who can think for themselves, criticize tradition, and understand the significance of another person's sufferings and achievements.

Conclusion

Did the students completing the Certificate of Personal and Professional Development affect the culture of Toshiba in a positive way? Students certainly demonstrated that they could use literature to address work-related problems. After the course ended, I asked the students as a group if they wanted to continue with the University courses (if money was no object). Emily appeared to answer for the group as a whole:

> Yes, definitely, because [this learning] gives people more confidence to tackle things they might not have had exposure to before. From what I've seen, we tackle situations better and in HR we are better about getting the right job role. We can now make an informed decision rather than just [giving] an opinion.

It is clear that work based learning at Toshiba has developed strong voices in the students. Moreover, they have learned to value their practical wisdom to make sound judgements in the absence of certainty. Being intellectually and morally sensitive to a situation as well as displaying courage, resilience and sound practical reasoning is what is valued highly by contemporary management. In my next chapter exploring the concept of leadership, the students at Wembley Stadium were expected to—and did—have these qualities as well as those at Toshiba. My role was to help them to articulate their experiences, wisdom and project plans through the use of literature.

References

Aristotle (2009) *The Nicomachean Ethics*. Translated by David Ross. Oxford: Oxford University Press.

Attridge, D. (2004). *The singularity of literature*. London: Routledge.

Baldwin, J. (1955). *Notes of a native son*. Boston: Beacon Press.

Barnett, R. (2004). *A will to learn*. Oxford: Oxford University Press.

Burnes, B. (2009). Reflections: Ethics and organizational change—time for a return to Lewinian values. *Journal of Change Management, 9*(4), 359–81.

Belfiore, E., & Upchurch, A. (Eds.). (2013). *Humanities in the twenty-first century. Beyond utility and markets*. London: Palgrave Macmillan.

Bérubé, M. (2013) The futility of the humanities. In E. Belfiore & A. Upchurch (Eds.), *Humanities in the Twenty-first Century. Beyond Utility and Markets.* London: Palgrave Macmillan.

Brookfield, S. (1987). *Developing critical thinkers—challenging adults to explore alternative ways of thinking and acting.* Milton Keynes: Open University Press.

Danielwicz, C. (2008). Personal genres, public voices. *NCTE, 59*(3), 420–50.

Deranty, J. P. (2008). Work in the precarisation of existence. *European Journal of Social Theory, 11*(4), 443–63.

Dewey, J. (2007). *How we think.* New York: Cosimo.

Eastman, C. A. (2013) The use of english literature in the context of work-based learning: A pedagogic case study. *Higher Education, Skills and Work-Based Learning, 3*(1), 62–72.

Eastman, C. A. (2014). English literature and work-based learning: A pedagogical case study. *International Journal of Lifelong Education, 32*(2), 141–160.

Edwards, A. (2010). *Being an expert professional practitioner: The relational turn in experience* (Vol. 3). Dortrecht: Springer.

Elbow, P. (2007). Voice in writing again: Embracing contraries. *College English, 70*(2), 168–88.

Ellnett, F. S, Jr. (2012). Practical rationality and a recovery of Aristotle's 'phronêsis'. In E. A. Kinsella & A. Pitman (Eds.), *Phronêsis as Professional Knowledge: Practical Wisdom in the Professions.* Rotterdam: Sense.

Gibbs, P. (2011). *Heidegger's contribution to the understanding of work-based studies.* Dortrecht: Springer.

Gibbs, P. (Ed.). (2013). *Learning work & practice: New understanding.* Dortrecht: Springer.

Hall, S. (2010). *Wisdom: From Philosophy to Neuroscience.* New York: Alfred A. Knopf.

Hinchcliff, G. (2013) Workplace, identity, transition and the role of learning. In Gibbs (Ed.) *Learning, Work and Practice: New Understandings.* Dortrecht: Springer.

Kemmis, S. (2012). Phronêsis, experience, and the primacy of praxis. In E. A. Kinsella & A. Pitman (Eds.), *Phronêsis as Professional Knowledge: Practical Wisdom in the Professions.* Rotterdam: Sense.

Kinsella, E. A., & Pitman, A. (Eds.). (2012). *Phronêsis as professional knowledge: Practical wisdom in the professions.* Rotterdam: Sense.

Kolb, D. (1984). *Experiential learning: Experience as the source of learning and development.* Englewood Cliffs: Prentice-Hall.

Lave, J., & Wenger, E. (1991). *Situated learning: Legitimate peripheral participation.* Cambridge: Cambridge University Press.

Lewin, K. (1935). *A dynamic theory of personality.* New York: McGraw-Hill.

Lewin, K. (1951). *Field theory in social science: Selected theoretical papers.* In D. Cartwright (Ed.). New York: Harper & Row.

Lewis, T. (2013). Tacit knowledge and the labour process. In P. Gibbs (Ed.), *Learning, Work & Practice.* Dortrecht: Springer.

Lum, G. (2013). The role of on-the-job and off-the-job provision in vocational education and training. In P. Gibbs (Ed.), *Learning, Work & Practice.* Dortrecht: Springer.

Marker, A. (2013). The development of practical wisdom: Its critical role in sustainable performance. *Performance Management, 52*(4), 11–21.

Molesworth, M., Nixon, E., & Scullion, R. (2009). Having, being and higher education: the marketization of the university and the transformation of the student into consumer. *Teaching in Higher Education, 14*(3), 277–287.

Nesi, H. (2012). Writing for the disciplines. In L. Clughen & C. Hardy (Eds.), *Writing in the disciplines: Building supportive cultures for student writing in UK higher education.* London: Emerald.

Nussbaum, M. (2010). *Not for profit.* Princeton: Princeton University Press.

Oxford English Dictionary (3rd Edn.) (2012) online.

Parker, J. (2013) Speaking out in a digital world: Humanities values, humanities processes. In E. Belfiore & A. Upchurch (Eds.), *Humanities in the Twenty-first Century. Beyond Utility and Markets.* London: Palgrave Macmillan.

Raelin, J. (2007). Toward an epistemology of practice. *The Academy of Management Learning and Education, 6*(4), 495–519.

Ryan, K., & Jenkins, C. (1997). On the loose—an interview with Robert Coles. *Journal of Education, 179*(3), 1–15.

Russell, R. (1996). *History of western philosophy*. Abingdon: Routledge.

Schön, D. (1991). *The reflective practitioner: How professionals think in action*. Aldershot: Ashgate.

Senge, P. (1990). *The dance of change—the challenges of sustaining momentum in learning organizations*. London: Nicholas Brearly.

Small, H. (2013). *The value of the humanities*. Oxford: Oxford University.

Speigelman, C. (2001). Argument and evidence in the case of the Persona. *College English., 64*(1), 63–87.

Sternberg, R. (2003). *Wisdom, intelligence and creativity synthesized*. Cambridge: Cambridge University.

West, T. (1996). Beyond dissensus exploring: Exploring the Heuristic value of conflict. *Rhetoric Review, 15*(11), 142–55.

Winch, C. (2013). The workplace as a site of learning: Reflections on the conceptual relationship between workplace and learning. In P. Gibbs (Ed.), *Learning, Work & Practice: New Understandings*. Dortrecht: Springer.

Chapter 3
The Quest for Leadership at Wembley Stadium

Who questions much, shall learn much, and retain much.
—Francis Bacon

Abstract A world leader in venue operation, Wembley Stadium is fully aware of the importance of its Crowd Safety and Security Managers and offers them training courses in a range of areas. The Stadium asked me to provide a course of advanced "training" to a group of students selected from among the team responsible for hundreds of security and steward staff. My brief was to help these students to recognise that they were high performing leaders that needed to inspire each other to become the best they could be. To this end, I introduced them to a selection of reading on leadership and helped them to put the ideas from their reading into practice. As one of the students put it, "I was attracted to the [leadership] course because I wanted to do better in my job. I have plenty of innovative ideas about how to run things here—I just need to know how to articulate them". Looking at theorists on leadership and ethics as well as seminal English essayists such as George Eliot and Francis Bacon, students were encouraged to re-examine the vague terms they had been using and to become more analytical and precise in their writing.

Introduction

Wembley Stadium (n.d.) claims to be a "world leader in venue operation". The Football Association is its primary stakeholder, and the Stadium hosts international football and rugby games, as well as music concerts and other sporting events. Events on this scale with thousands of spectators entail complex safety and security needs to ensure the safety of Wembley's customers and to enable the Stadium to achieve its stated mission of "exceed[ing] customer expectations". Wembley's Crowd Safety and Security managers have a pivotal role to play in the Stadium's operations. Wembley recognises the importance of these managers and, to this end, offers them

© The Author(s) 2016
C.A. Eastman, *Improving Workplace Learning by Teaching Literature*,
SpringerBriefs in Education, DOI 10.1007/978-3-319-29028-7_3

training courses in a range of areas: first aid; disengagement and physical intervention; door supervision; CCTV and radio operations; managing events safely.

In the autumn of 2012 when I began to work with the students based at Wembley, the Stadium wanted to enhance its training offering to these managers. A group of nine were selected from among the team responsible for hundreds of security and steward staff at the Stadium. These students worked at Wembley on a part-time basis and had primary jobs in the Civil Service, UK Armed Forces, teaching and charities.[1] At Wembley they managed highly pressurised situations involving the public safety of up to 95,000 people including employees and spectators, and their local decision making skills had to be of the highest order. Furthermore, their leadership underpinned the safe and effective operation of this international Stadium. According to Peter Swordy, the then head of Wembley's Centre of Excellence for whom the students worked, Middlesex University was seen as a local and efficient partner, capable of delivering "all of the requirements set out in the brief". I delivered a Personal and Professional Development module (the same as the one for Toshiba), except that my focus with Wembley was on leadership. I ran two two-hour seminars on-site and conducted the rest of the course on Skype with individual students.

The Wembley students were different from the Toshiba cohort in that they were composed of students of varying degrees of exposure to higher education. Whereas no students from the Toshiba cohort had any university experience, two of the students from Wembley had, and were consequently quite confident academically: they knew the basics of citation, referencing and research. Given the varying educational backgrounds of the students and the fact that some of the group felt intimidated by their more academic peers, I took the decision to supplement the group work with individually tailored one-to-one sessions, in which I could meet the students' learning needs more effectively. For Docherty (2011, p. 51) learning equates to the "release of potential". My students at Wembley were in danger of becoming disheartened by feeling the need constantly to measure up to their peers. Their learning threatened to fall short of the transformative experience envisaged by Docherty. After the first class a few students approached me to confide in me their fears of being "not as clever" as the two who had been to university. They admitted to a sense of "exclusion" because they did not think they could express themselves as well as the other two students.

I have always seen group work as one of the crucial dynamics to the success of a student cohort, and I have noted a correlation between participation on virtual learning environments and doing well academically. Therefore, I urged all the students to post their contributions on the activity board and engage with each other as much as possible on this virtual learning space. I decided to provide Skype sessions to the students which were targeted particularly at the less confident students, but were also available to the more confident students. If, according to my brief, students were expected to become "high performing leaders who understand their roles and responsibilities and continually inspire each other to be the best they can be",

---

[1]Their principal jobs ranged from fairly significant managerial roles to entry level positions perhaps reflecting the subsequent comments by the students on the range of abilities at Wembley.

I needed them to be open to their own possibilities and not to be compromised by these initial fantasies of inferiority. I saw myself as someone who could bring out all of the students' innate wisdom, supporting them to reach far beyond the confines of the prescribed module.

"The Graduate"

In his criticism on what he calls the vacuous concept of "knowledge-transfer", Docherty (2011, p. 41) points out that we do not communicate by "transferring the content of one consciousness into another". We need to be alert to the fact that there is no such module that contains "the knowledge that we can either teach or learn" (p. 41). Instead I saw my role as providing the tools—to demonstrate how to cite and reference, how to find substantiating evidence in the research, how to read critically and write with a purpose. The students were the experts on leadership—I was simply the guide. One of the students, Andy explains:

> At first I thought there wouldn't be anything from the course that was directly relevant to what I was doing and am still doing at Wembley. I didn't think there would be anything directly relevant and then I learned about different styles of leadership. This was absolutely vital. It allowed me to view my own leadership skills but also leadership skills and traits of others. So I was able to re-affirm my own leadership traits and to adjust them to whatever setting I was in. I could modify my leadership traits more subtly to fit in around all situations.

I could not teach Andy to be a leader. Leadership was a quality he had to discover for himself. As Warren Bennis astutely observes, the essence of leadership is being oneself and being able to express oneself freely: "The man is only half himself, the other half his expression" (Ralph Waldo Emerson in Bennis 1989, p. 2). All I could do was put at Andy's disposal the theoretical literature on leadership to enable him to reflect on his own leadership style. Leadership is not a "knowledge" that can be "transferred"; leadership is a skill crafted in Andy's day-to-day practice, a skill that can be enhanced by exploring the relevant literature. Bennis formulates a notion of leadership distilled from Emerson's reflections on the role of self-reliance in forging one's position in society. In his study of leadership, Bennis makes the point that leaders have traditionally made the time to reflect. I would have liked to have introduced two of Emerson's contemporaries into the mix, Henry David Thoreau and Herman Melville, but time did not permit a digestion of these great writers that would have done them justice.[2]

---

[2]With a group of software engineers, I am currently using excerpts from Thoreau's *Walden* and Melville's *Moby-Dick* to explore the concept of leadership from a literary perspective, questioning concepts of appreciative observation, non-conformity and the tensions between the individual and authority.

Tim said something similar to Andy:

> When I am in an explosive or controversial situation like a situation between two conflicting
> groups of spectators I think I have now gained the ability to be more objective and not to be
> directly affected by a situation. I can stand back now and actually assess what is the best
> course of action and then move forward gradually rather than diving straight in without
> thinking.

Experiencing the reading they did, particularly on leadership, provided the students with a legitimising power. As Docherty (2011, p. 55) reminds us: "the very point of learning is to gain authority through the transformations that constitute learning". It is clear to me that the students were eager to construct a new configuration of their knowledge: they thought they knew certain things about leadership, indeed they did have a deep knowledge of leadership derived from their practice at Wembley. What they needed was to vindicate this knowledge using external authorities in a bid to establish ownership of their ideas. Authority is what I needed to instil in my students. Authority is what the work based learning programme could offer already competent professionals.

Docherty (2011, p. 57) laments an economic model that precludes innovation, as businesses comfortably perpetuate the status quo, fuelled by indifferent graduates who act as receptacles for the received wisdom of the companies in which they start to work:

> once they have graduated, students find it difficult to exercise their authority in the work-
> place. Corporate business – the graduate's employer – has nothing to learn from our grad-
> uates; on the contrary, the graduates have everything to learn from the business in question.
> Is it any surprise that business routinely complains that Universities do not provide the
> specific qualities that business requires? The one thing that business does not require is the
> authority of its workforce to change things: conformity and regulation – efficiency – is again
> the dominant code.

Undergraduates' authority is stifled by rigid university syllabi that restrict independent thought, and their authority, once they have graduated, continues to be silenced by workplaces that seem to require, all too often, the conformity of staff as cogs in the machine of economic efficiency. Universities and workplaces create, in Docherty's view, a self-perpetuating cycle of mediocrity and stagnation. Students are not allowed to exercise their authority in the workplace, nor are they trained to exercise it by universities. Yet some businesses are eager to break out of the routine of established practice; they yearn to find new ways of doing things. Wembley was one of these businesses. But the Stadium needed a means of giving their staff the authority to effect real change: work based learning was to provide this means.

To contextualise Docherty's claim regarding the unhealthy and unproductive relationship between universities and the workplace, we have to bear in mind that Docherty is examining the "myth" of "student experience" and the paradox that instead of encouraging freedom and autonomy for students, the "student experience" is a model of mechanised encounters with higher education, dreamed up by university marketing managers: teaching and learning have become an "appended afterthought"; they have "now explicitly become the least important priorities for the future development of 'the student experience'" (p. 65).

I quote Docherty's less than complimentary remarks about the commercialisation, marketisation and institutional mind-set that, according to him, have shaped the university sector not because I disagree or agree with him—although he makes valid points particularly when he discusses the need to consider learning and teaching rooted in genuine encounters between academic staff and students hungry to learn and explore knowledge autonomously. I quote him, especially his opinion on the divergence between the graduate profile businesses think they are looking for and the actual graduates who could make a difference to these businesses, because my work with Wembley demonstrates how this divergence need not be the rule. Some businesses—enlightened businesses—want to learn from their employees and look to the authority of its workforce to effect change. They ask universities for help in drawing out their employees' wisdom so that they can develop the best possible workforce. The experience of real life and real learning "devalued" in preference to "schemes drawn up in the classroom that are supposed to capture the reality of that external world" (p. 43) is the antithesis of what a progressive company like Wembley wanted to achieve.

When I asked Peter Swordy how he would measure the success of the programme on leadership I delivered to the security managers, he told me that "the climate of the Stadium team was enhanced, and, using metrics through a partner of Visit England [the official tourist board of England], [we] established that staff performance has improved game on game through qualitative analysis and also customer feedback to satisfaction surveys".

There is corporate business that recognises it can learn from students. Through a tailored programme of work based learning not only is it possible to capture the authority of the workforce to effect positive change, it is, from my experience, safe to say that the business has everything to learn from the students. Work based learning students have no brief with conformity. If anything, they have been in the workforce long enough to experience how liberating critical thinking is and how deadening and soul-destroying going along with a kind of herd mentality can be. As Carrie put it: "I was attracted to the course because I wanted to do better in my job. I have plenty of innovative ideas about how to run things here—I just need how to articulate them."

The psychologist Robert Sternberg (Sternberg and Lubart 1995, p. 5) states that intelligence serves three key roles in creativity: synthetic, analytic and practical. This third aspect of intelligence: "the ability effectively to present one's work to an audience"; the reaching beyond "the status quo in one's field" and seeing things in fresh, "unentrenched" ways are aspects of intelligence that a business like Wembley was looking for in their staff. Through two informal face-to-face seminars, the aforementioned Skype sessions and an on-line discussion forum, I encouraged the students to read widely in the field of leadership theory, particularly from Joanne Ciulla's study on leadership effectiveness and ethics, as well as from other theorists in the field of leadership and ethics such as Robert Solomon, Bernard Bass and Paul

Steidlmeier. I also introduced the students to writing from 19th century essayists to examine whether more "literary" literature would be helpful for their learning.[3]

Background

Throughout this chapter I will be concerned with the examination of a transformation of self. If transformation is indeed at the heart of any serious university education, I aim to demonstrate the possibility of student transformation with the Wembley cohort. In order to give some background to the work I did with Wembley, I need to point out that my time with the students was brief—seven months. Despite its brevity, my work with the Wembley cohort informs a narrative which should illuminate some fundamental principles on getting the best out of students in terms of improving their writing, critical thinking skills and reflective abilities through the use of literature. Moreover, my research in this chapter addresses the widespread and urgent concerns about the state of the university (Collini 2011; Docherty 2011; Nussbuam 2010; Readings 1996; Said 1994). I contend that part of the solution to the crisis in teaching and learning lies in adopting a work based curriculum that privileges literature. If, as Docherty (2011, p. 4) asserts, there has been an anti-university mood in the UK (and other Western countries) for the past few decades coupled with the poisonous after taste of an historical legacy in which the university is "construed as a site of privilege" especially of "class privilege", I would argue that the only way to address this culture of "mistrust" and revive "a certain sense of purpose" is to get more businesses to work with universities. If the biggest threat to universities is the poten-tial triumph of "banality" and "blandness" (Docherty 2011, p. 23), maybe the entrée into university needs to be *from work*, rather than the path from university *to work*.

Said (1994, p. xii) writes that it is important to take a risk "in order to go beyond the easy certainties provided to us by our background, language, nationality, which so often shield us from the reality of others". Perhaps if universities found more of their students from a pool of those already working, already exposed to corporate thinking, already keen to find their own voices, they would be discovering the kind of student who, in questioning authority, continues to pursue the common good. As Said makes clear, one of the main intellectual activities of the past century has been "the questioning, not to say undermining of authority" (p. 67). Companies that are unafraid of their employees' questioning, even undermining authority in a construc-tive fashion, have the most to gain from a university alliance. Tim articulated his concern about how present security operations were run:

> It was important for me to learn how to reference because I would then substantiate what I was saying with some authority. I have always had strong opinions on how things needed

---

[3]See Chap. 1 for my discussion of Attridge's distinction between literary literature and instrumen-talist literature.

to be run. It was crucial to find quotations and reading to make my points stronger and to challenge the present state of security operations.

For Tim, gaining the tools to make concrete and authoritative an already strong opinion was the means to challenge corporate decision making. This questioning, challenging, even constructive undermining of authority leads to better decision making by a better informed staff. Before taking part in the programme, Tim evidently felt his voice carried little weight. His increased confidence, after being exposed to the critical literature, is evident in his testimony.

Leadership at Wembley

The students had to complete three writing tasks as part of their personal and professional development module. They were supposed to review the short course that a trainer had delivered to them (on coaching and mentoring, management styles, leadership and empowering staff), produce a personal and professional development plan and, finally, evaluate how other people help them develop in work. The following is an excerpt from Eric's first task, the review of the short course:

> Whilst the course explored various methods in coaching and mentoring, it also emphasised the importance as a manager in understanding what coaching and mentoring actually mean and how approaches can be used to develop staff. Sadly I don't think the majority of attendees understood the concept at the beginning of the course and some had little concept of how to put it in practice at the end. This is not a reflection on the trainer but more on an indication of the selection of attendees, which future courses could maybe address via more effective pre-course reading and engagement.

Eric is commenting on the concept of a "community of practice" falling short of its ideals. I was not the trainer who delivered the short courses at Wembley, so I am unable to comment on the content and quality of the provision. However, the training was delivered as part of a work based learning programme, so my comments on work based learning ought to be valid here. Raelin (2007, p. 77) discusses the importance of identity in work based learning, stating that learning who one is, recognising one's identity, is inevitable: "who one takes oneself to be emerges and retreats in fluid, variable experiences, typically at work, but also in all aspects of life—in the home, the community, and the nation-state". Eric perceives his identity as divorced from "the majority" of the group and diagnoses a pre-course of reading as an antidote to failed learning experience. Although he does not use the expression, he perceives that "a community of practice" is being severely compromised. Eric further comments:

> In my experience any organisation is only as good as its employees. The successful ones place strong emphasis on personal attributes in selecting and developing staff. However, this does not come without challenges: not least of which may be gaps in the experience, knowledge, attitudes, skills, behaviours or leadership required to perform demanding roles. Formal training courses may be able to bridge some knowledge/skills gaps but employees will more

often than not develop faster and further with dedicated guidance that inspires, energises and facilitates.

This sounds to me like Joe Raelin's "black box of co-op", a secret recipe that seems to give some work based learners a distinct advantage over others. Raelin points to the confidence and self-efficacy that emerge from individuals working together and making judgements that are "embedded in the sociability of the work environment" (p. 508). Those gaps in "experience, knowledge, attitudes, skills, behaviours or leadership" occur when a community of practice—the informal and formal collaboration between those with shared goals—is not evident. I discovered a pattern of discontent among the Wembley students regarding how the training courses were implemented. Nikki commented that many of the managers did not know what was required of them in terms of leading a team: "during our group work we were all given different role play scenarios to do with leadership. People kept struggling to work together and they couldn't develop resolution as a team." Ron noted that managers really struggled with letting their staff make decisions: "they were afraid to delegate responsibility even in role play scenarios." Paula wrote that she could see that "too many people wanted assurance from their peers that different practices like delegating work and empowering staff were acceptable practices." The students did not realise that they could delegate work and empower staff: they did not understand the basics of leadership. They were given tasks to play in a vacuous role-play environment and they thought they had to play according to the rules of the game rather than according to the rules of the world of work. There was a divorce between theory and praxis: the two were not integrated for any useful learning to emerge.

If we accept that a community of practice is likely to enhance a company's profitability by helping it to resolve problems expeditiously (Raelin 2007), then, in Eric's words, successful companies need to "place strong emphasis on personal attributes, in selecting and developing staff". Additionally, employees need training that fosters a sense of community built on reflection on current practice. It is simply not good enough to construct artificial and pre-packaged "play" to use Docherty's (2011, p. 57) word and thereby restrain teaching and learning. Pre-packaged course materials that do not take into account the needs of individual students "[arrest] the development from play into learning". When I met with the students for ther discussion quickly turned to leadership. They saw value in the short term courses but wanted guidance on how to transform their group into a true community of practice. I reassured the ones who considered themselves less academically able than their peers that I would be present for them and that we would all work together, not competing against each other but strengthening their own work place identity by examining leadership at Wembley as part of a programme of work place learning. If we revisit Gibbs' (2011, p. 21) definition of work place learning as learning about "engaging in the workplace and understanding how to move around and use the tools of that workplace" reaching to a future possibility of "mastery, expertise or, indeed, phronêsis (practical wisdom)", we can clearly discern some of the students' initial frustration with the training sessions populated by people who did not understand how to move around and use the tools of the workplace: Eric and the others experienced disunity and even amateurishness.

In my subsequent discussions on leadership and conformity, I will demonstrate how phronêsis was encouraged at Wembley. If professions are "plagued", as Kinsella and Pitman (2012, p. 4) assert, "with a theory-practice gap", I think that what the Wembley students achieved looks a lot like "reflection oriented toward phronêsis" within professional practice.

Leadership and Ethics

One of the themes that emerged consistently in students' discussions of where they thought their current training provision was falling short was leadership. To address the dearth of theoretical writing the students were being exposed to, I introduced them first to Ciulla's (2004) chapter "Ethics & Leadership Effectiveness". Coming from a philosophical background, Ciulla uses a combination of case studies and seminal works by the Ancient Greeks, particularly Aristotle, and Renaissance thinkers such as Machiavelli to explore ageless questions on justice, virtue and duty, as well as offering a breadth of views and unique insights on the scholarship of leadership. Her work covers the history of and current practices in ethics and leadership as well as poses profound questions which I thought the students could engage with in discussion groups on-line after looking at their work in class. From reading Ciulla, they might, for example, ponder whether ethical leaders are driven by self-interest or which actions serve the greatest good.

Because leadership theory now underpins a wealth of material on organisational change, I wanted the students to read widely on leadership. Moreover, because more and more companies are interested in providing training programmes in leadership or in designing ethical codes for their employees, I chose Ciulla's work as a lucid and interesting introduction into this complex area. In "Ethics & Leadership Effectiveness" Ciulla (2004) poses two related questions at the centre of leadership research: What is leadership? What is good leadership?

In the first face to face meeting students approached a definition of leadership in negative terms, by telling me what it was not. It was not about "neglecting and disincentivising your staff". It was not about "abdicating responsibility" or "struggling to delegate". Weeks into the course many of the students were now able to problematise leadership by highlighting issues from their primary jobs. Here is Eric discussing the prison service:

> I have seen many different leadership initiatives come and go, from a truly militaristic positional power approach based on rank, through to the current approach of participatory democracy, whereby the leader holds the position via distribution of responsibility, empowerment (of team members) and aiding rather than directing deliberations. I now see why this second approach works better. As Ciulla (2004) points out, leadership is about human relationships and the moral responsibility to work democratically.

Holly considered her primary job as a housing officer:

Eliot (1991) lauds Thomas Carlyle, stating that he is an example of the most effective kind of writer, one who doesn't discover things about himself but 'rouses in others' the desire for them to discover. Eliot believes that a good writer not only convinces people of an idea and gets them to consider right and wrong but will get them to seek out what needs to be sought out. She supports her main points with evidence which is exactly what I have learned to do. If I can persuade my staff and shareholders that getting someone into a financial advice role would be beneficial for the organisation – that would be good. Even better, if I can rouse energy in the staff and get them to come up with their own ideas, everyone feels a part of the whole. Likewise, I need to do this at Wembley. I've learned from Eliot to be precise when presenting my ideas, selecting my main points and supporting my observations with evidence. I've learned not only how to present the advantages of a situation – say, on how we should address leadership here – but also on the disadvantages of a situation, making sure I counter-argue as Eliot does.

In addition to offering students Ciulla's work on leadership and ethics, I provided them with examples from essays such as Eliot's in order to illustrate the mechanics of constructing an argument. Most students preferred the more contemporary writers such as Ciulla and Solomon probably because they did not have the time to grasp the more antiquated style of the 19th century essayists such as George Eliot and earlier essayists such as Francis Bacon. However, in writing about good leadership, Holly was able to integrate both Ciulla's "Great Man" theory of leadership—"the Hitler Problem"—and Francis Bacon's ideas into her argument.

I first introduced the students to Ciulla's "Great Man" theory in class. I broached this topic by asking the students to define good leadership. Predictably, some of the students claimed that good leaders in history could be easily recognised because they were "great men". They cited figures like Winston Churchill, Abraham Lincoln, and Mahatma Gandhi. "What about Adolf Hitler?" I asked them provocatively. Many of the students laughed; some were perplexed. There was a serious point behind my provocation. Ciulla calls this the Hitler paradox: can bad men be good leaders? Many of the students found it impossible to reconcile the idea of good leadership with Hitler. Did the epithet "good" when applied to "leadership" imply that leaders have to be moral? Hitler was an effective leader, some of the students claimed, but that was not necessarily the same thing as being a "good" leader. By exposing the students to Ciulla's theory I was able to get them to think more deeply about what they understood by the term "good leadership". They were able to move beyond citing examples of individuals they thought were good leaders and they began to analyse the concept itself.

Some of the most eloquent reflection on leadership was offered by Holly in the written work she produced following the class, in which she was able to support her own analysis with an evaluation of the work of diverse thinkers. Holly explained that the problem with focusing on "The Great Man" as a useable model of leadership investigation was that although Hitler was a charismatic leader, he was immoral, even amoral:

Hitler was totally unethical and definitely not a great leader because of his tremendous flaws. Ciulla (2004, p. 38) reminds us that he was a "bully". My research and reading have made me reflect naturally on the type of leadership we have at Wembley. Certainly not in Hitler's case (because he was a political tyrant and could exercise total power), I think that we over-estimate the impact of leaders. When things are going well, that person is considered a good or even great leader. When things go wrong, the leader is considered incompetent and even worse. I've seen people use the excuse of bad leadership to take advantage of the system. Some people feel as though they are getting even with senior management for some imagined transgressions. What Francis Bacon (1983) says about revenge – you can get even with an enemy (senior management) - but you would be a superior person if you let it go resonates with my experiences at work. Bacon's advice can therefore be easily adapted to the work-place. Recently there were management changes taking place that were definitely affecting staff morale. Questions were raised about my own competency but I was patient and refused to engage. To date, I hold no grudges against these people and I feel I can hold my head high.

Ciulla (2004, p. 304) contends that the humanities "provide a larger context in which we can synthesise what we know about leadership". Leadership studies and work based learning appear to be a natural fit because both take knowledge from a range of disciplines, both are interdisciplinary. The students were able to analyse leadership literature from psychology, business studies and political science, and they were also witnesses to how leadership as a subject can be consolidated by inte-grating reading from the humanities: "more scholars from the humanities have entered the field, and more leadership scholars are doing interdisciplinary work. This is a substantial development because the humanities give us a different knowledge than do the sciences and social sciences" (Ciulla 2004, p. 304).

Like leadership studies, work based learning is interdisciplinary. The breadth of work based learning as a practice provides ample space for borrowing from different disciplines. Brennan (2003) defines work based learning simply as learning arising from activity in the workplace. Connor (2005) defines it as knowledge in the work-place including workforce development. King (2007, p. 28) specifies that work based learning programmes are initiated by demand from employers or employees, and have "learning outcomes linked to business performance outcomes". Because work based learning is learning positioned within a working context and derived from the workplace, our students inevitably come from diverse backgrounds: students are expected to strive for innovative and ground-breaking research using knowledge from their sector as well as from academic disciplines such as engineering, education, social work, computer sciences, medicine and business. Nevertheless, there seems to have been a tacit understanding that a work based learning student's research would be confined, for the most part, to social and natural sciences. Ciulla's point about the humanities not being a site of investigation into leadership until recently has implications in work based learning. I contend that we need the humanities for understanding more about work and learning in work. Holly's acute analysis of leadership based on her consideration of a range of literary and theoretical texts illustrates the usefulness of integrating the humanities into a work based learning curriculum. One would not generally expect to find reflections on Francis Bacon's essays in the work of a student interrogating the concept of leadership, but Holly's use of Francis Bacon gives a richness to her arguments: she has harnessed the wisdom of centuries old philosophers. She is applying sage knowledge derived from literature to her current practice which surely is the essence of phronêsis.

Ciulla (2004, p. 8) observes that what is considered leadership literature emerges primarily from the fields of psychology, business and political science: "the scarcity of work done on leadership in the humanities is another reason why there is little done on ethics". Through exposure to numerous "training" sessions, the students were able to discuss leadership but had not been exposed to any reading on the moral implications of leadership. I recognised that they were comfortable discussing coaching, mentoring, types of leadership styles and management strategies. Up to this point, they had not been introduced to any literature from the humanities on ethics which Ciulla insists is integral to "understanding" (p. 14) leadership.

In their first tentative posts on-line before we had our first session exploring leadership in detail, students wrote about leadership without the requisite ethical layers that could develop into a far more complex and textured portrait:

> The GROW model (goal, reality, options, will) can be used as a checklist to enhance leadership skills.
>
> Leadership can be developed faster and further with dedicated guidance.
>
> The main part of leadership is to help develop, support and coach my staff.
>
> Good leadership will show your members of staff growing into their careers.
>
> As a manager and leader, I have always been conscious of how my behaviour and management style reflect on the performance of my team.
>
> Although there are many schools of thought on what traits the most effective leaders display, in reality the most effective leaders are the ones that have the ability to switch between styles depending on a situation.

There is nothing mistaken with their comments on leadership. In fact, they were all able to explain different leadership styles and argue for the advantages and against the disadvantages of each. However, when I introduced Ciulla's Hitler problem to them, the ethical aspects of leadership, hitherto unexplored, altered their ideas about leadership, making the concept richer and suddenly more fundamental to the nature of the experience of being human. The students had been looking at leadership from a systemic perspective, one in which "the leadership role is one factor in an intricate system of interacting elements which affect how leadership is best applied in organisation settings and how it can be improved" (Tate 2012, p. 1). There is nothing inherently wrong with common models that employ a range of management theories to help people better understand leadership. In fact, there is a great deal to learn from improving a management paradigm by reflecting on ways to avoid the "silo" mentality, defining a standard of what successful leadership looks like and making people more co-operative, accountable and interdependent (Tate 2012). It is reasonable to assume that any kind of model which promotes "good leadership" should develop the capabilities and shape the behaviour of all those involved in organisational life. Integrating ethics into the study of leadership, however, is essential in supporting students to understand the fundamental difference between leadership and "good" leadership.

In the Aristotelian sense, ethics is moral virtue. Aristotle (2009, p. 90) dismisses the excesses and deficiencies of passions characterised, for example, by envy and spite and empty vanity and undue humility and other passions that have no mean and should simply be avoided. He settles on this definition: virtue "is a state of character concerned with choice, lying in a mean". Mean for Aristotle is the area between excess and deficiency. Perhaps leadership or responsibility for other people necessitates an avoidance of excess or of deficiency and instead aims for a golden mean: the virtuous person has the appropriate emotions to act the right way. Not only did an ethical exploration of leadership enrich the students' discussions and writing, it helped them to progress from explaining leadership to understanding it.

At first the students were more inclined to adhere to the "surface" qualities of leadership, discussing distributive leadership, the problems of hierarchical leadership and leadership as a resource. Exploring ethics deepened any surface understanding of the topic. For example, they started to interrogate the role of charisma in leadership. At the outset of the course, some students appeared to consider Hitler a "great" leader. Students who have not been exposed to the study of ethics focus on his influence over history, his all-encompassing power over his followers and his ability to shape the goals and purposes of his organisation (the country of Germany). However, as their reading progressed, it was clear that their reading had helped them to identify a more thorough definition and manifest a more rigorous understanding of leadership. In addition to the introductory Ciulla chapter, students read essays from other leadership theorists. From Andy's reading of Robert Solomon:

> Like Solomon (2004), I am convinced the moral leader is essential for any good organisation. I found it intriguing that he claimed the reason why these days we can't find extraordinary leaders like Churchill or Lincoln is that we don't want one. I think we need to be wary of qualities like charisma because we then start to think about leadership emotionally and link charismatic leaders with mystery and magic.

I think it would be useful to quote Solomon at some length because so many of the students paraphrased this section of his essay:

> I argue that charisma is not anything in particular. It is not a distinctive quality of personality or character, and it is not an essential implement of leadership. Rather it is a misleading even if exciting concept that deflects us from the emotional complexity of leadership that might better occupy our attention. Charisma is not a single quality, not is it a single emotion or set of emotions. It is a generalized way of pointing to and emptily explaining an emotional relationship that is readily characterised as fascination but should be analysed more fundamentally in terms of trust (Ciulla 2004, p. 91).

Elsewhere I have detailed the kind of unchallenging SWOT and PEST analyses on which they are expected to comment. Yet all the students rose to the challenge of engaging with the essayists in Ciulla's edited book on leadership and ethics, an accomplishment to which I attribute two reasons. First, work based learners must be given the opportunity to select what they know is important in their practice and second, they must be guided in the simple techniques of close reading. The former consideration allows me to return to Barnett's (2007, p. 17) discussion on having a will to learn. He posits that students are motivated less by rationality and more by the irrationality that is "interior to the person". This idea of interiority is akin to identity. As part-time employees at the Stadium, the students had all undergone the usual vicissitudes of any job, but as a group, were focused on the problems and challenges of leadership for the organisation. They had described a recent situation when a group of boisterous fans had charged a barrier and, without quick thinking and in one of their words "strong leadership", catastrophe could have ensued. The students had invested in themselves as leaders: their very identity was interlinked with leadership. As Barnett puts it, when a student invests in himself deeply, he is investing in himself "as a person": the student is "giving of himself in a first-hand way" (p. 18). My work with all students recognises the crucial role that identity has in practitioners' lives.

To turn now to the second consideration of emphasising the techniques of close reading, I would define this process as one which demands that the reader analyses text in fine detail. The reader needs to ask: What is the first thing I notice about this passage? What are the key words? What is the writer's point of view? What imagery is used? What symbolism is used? Are there any metaphors? Through close and attentive care to the kind of writing in which students were interested, they started to see that many terms that were reiterated in their training sessions needed to be deconstructed fully. For example, one of their short training sessions was on "empowerment". I asked them to consider whether "empowering" employees neces-sarily changed the balance of power within an organisation. I suggested as a corollary that empowerment had to be closely aligned with responsibility. In order to under-stand fully what lies behind the concept of "empowerment", it is incumbent upon us as teachers to explore ethics with students.

The training sessions that the Wembley students had been attending did not encourage the students to analyse the vague terms they were using. At the beginning of our course when the students discussed "empowerment" on-line, their arguments were punctuated with phrases such as "an important skill", "a way of achieving your overall aim", "helping staff make decisions", "an essential consideration in the toolbox of another manager". There was little attempt to go beyond the definition or a superficial description of a word or phrase. By the end of the course, the students recognised that the ethical dimensions of their practice were germane to any consid-ered discussion. They began to look at leadership as multi-faceted, a "many-headed hydra", and took the point that Bass and Steidlmeier (2004, p. 175) make that lead-ership ethics must take in one's moral character, the values embedded in one's vision and the morality of actions one pursues. The students' work started to take on depth:

I wanted to develop a real team ethos of supporting each other so that whilst my team members are responsible for specific parts of a whole world package, they will start to become aware of the very real benefits of working together. This may appear a very basic need, but I knew I lacked mutual support within the team. I knew it was essential to engender mutual trust, loyalty and commitment within the people I was responsible for. I needed to create the right team environment by looking to inspire, challenge and lead by example. Bass and Steidlmeier (2004) claim that our values have to be embedded in our vision. My vision needed to be clear and it also needed to be communicated easily. My team had been de-motivated and didn't have a great deal of self-worth. As a leader, I have to challenge them to improve and develop as I demonstrate my own improvement and development.

The student's narrative started to take on a degree of criticality previously absent. Naturally, this transformation, first at reflection and writing level, then at an actual performance level is not easy. However, the students' conclusion that authentic transformation leaders, the leaders that they were aspiring to be, leaders that were "morally uplifting and even manipulative 'for the common good'" needed to be at the heart of the Wembley leadership enterprise (Bass and Steidlmeier 2004, p. 179). This transformation in thought or deed is, as I stated, not an easy process. Some of the students were reluctant readers and writers, a difficulty compounded by the fact that they had been suppressed by the dead hand of conventional thinking and conformity. To coax out their independent spirits, their sense of going against conventional wisdom, I needed to encourage them to trust their practical wisdom, the phonêsis that lies in all dedicated practitioners.

Leadership and Creativity

Sternberg and Lubart (1995, p. vii) claim that "creativity, like intelligence, is something that everyone possesses in some amount. Moreover, creativity is not a fixed attribute: a person's level of creativity is not carved in stone at birth, and like any talent, it is something virtually anyone can develop in varying degrees". We either are a convert to this way of thinking or not. Sternberg and Lubart relate numerous anecdotes and stories to persuade the reader that intelligence is not enough. We need creativity, that is to "go against the crowd in effective ways" to succeed in life (p. vii). They use the analogy of the stock market in their insistence that people need to be wise investors in the "marketplace" of ideas as well as risk takers, defining creativity as the generation of ideas that are "novel, appropriate, and of high quality" (p. 2). They point out that business schools do not prepare students for the real world of business. Learning "sophisticated quantitative techniques" or "a case study method" for resolving work based (or indeed any kinds of) problems is not what a business requires (p. 16). The only way to stay competitive is to think innovatively:

> Our culture is risk-averse. Even some of our most cherished proverbs – a bird in the hand is worth two in the bush, or a penny saved is a penny earned – imply risk aversion. If we wish to encourage creativity, we need to rethink our generalized cultural values and teach children from an early age to take the risks that can potentially lead to creative work (p. 51).

The authors stress that risk aversion is prevalent among most organisations—most people fear offending superiors so keep ideas to themselves. Wembley Stadium then needs to be congratulated for wanting to hear what its employees think, for valuing their ideas on leadership, for advocating non-conformist unorthodox solutions to problems. Students assessed some of the current management practices at the time:

> Falling achievement due to a rigid hierarchy.

Fundamental differences between management and leadership have not been addressed thus far.

We've been doing things in the same way for a long time and need to re-examine our long standing practices.

The students' research into creative ways of finding new leadership models at the Stadium was positively encouraged. We know that in the field of leadership development the conventional classroom epistemology dictates that managers exit the workplace for the classroom. They stop being managers and "learn" to be students (Bolden and Gosling 2006). To my mind, this practice is counterintuitive. Work based learning students are not subjected to a sharp delineation between work and learning: learning is an aspect of work and businesses such as Wembley that promote this concept are those that take on a fundamental role in leadership development for their staff. My experience with the Wembley students convinced me that work based learning students do not need so much to question their assumptions about leadership or to be challenged to think about different leadership models. They are all creative enough to imagine what "good" leadership looks like: they simply need the tools to fashion their arguments as coherently as possible.

Stories and Public Voices

One of the most creative approaches to the seemingly insurmountable problems within one team was from Carrie who used a narrative approach to redefine the problem. Put simply, no one seemed to be taking personal responsibility for things when they went wrong. As she articulated it:

Giving everyone in my team particular duties and responsibilities was what I initially thought was the right course of action to take. However, the more I challenged them to deliver, the less they did. I even tried to have regular team meetings where I encouraged everyone to be honest – to have an open line of communication. Attitudes failed to change, and, in fact, my team was becoming harder and harder to manage. Someone even suggested I was passing the buck in terms of giving them responsibility for what I was supposed to be doing.

Her narrative continues as she relates her growing frustration and even anger until she comes up with an idea. She decides to delegate leadership responsibilities to each member of the team in turn. She finds the situation turns around because staff seem to be more inclined to work harder for these "temporary" bosses: they know that their turns will come next and they work effectively because they have a vested interest in demonstrating their capability as leaders. My first point is that Carrie thought creatively in her real-world leadership challenge. Second, she told a story: "stories help make concrete the various phenomena we are studying" (Sternberg and Lubart 1995, p. 100). By narrativising her experience, Carrie was laying the groundwork for future conduct; she was ensuring she would not make the same mistakes in future.

The authors maintain that much of creativity lies in storytelling. Waterhouse (2007) maintains that leadership is invariably problematic. We think of its domain as belonging to the few, to the elite, to have a formal and authoritative shape. Yet as Carrie related, there was another side to it: it could be perceived as a behaviour nearly anyone, temporarily, can adopt. Waterhouse (2007, p. 272) sees stories of leadership emerging as modes that "illuminate the lived experiences of leadership". Although her specific focus is on leadership narratives in school settings, Waterhouse makes a valuable point about how we use stories to make sense of our own experiences. I encouraged the students to tell their stories within the auto-ethnographic tradition as defined by the pioneer auto-ethnographers Ellis and Bochner (2000, p. 739) as "a genre of writing and research that displays multiple layers of consciousness, connecting the personal to the cultural". Ellis and Bochner underscore the importance of placing the student researcher at the centre of his or her own story. The student is on a journey to understand herself and others as well as attempting to be self questioning and self analytical and not to be overly concerned about objectivity. Naturally we want students to ground their narratives in facts and evidence, but personal identity and the ability to make sense of our working lives are so integral to work based learning that we cannot escape the meaning constructed through the telling of one's story. As Barnett (2007, p. 94) asserts, confidence emerges from finding one's own voice and we, as teachers, must do everything in our power to encourage the learner's voice and the learner's story:

> Higher education does much to suppress voice. It unduly censures; it places tight boundaries of 'disciplines' around students' thoughts; it asserts itself in hierarchical pedagogical relationships; it even belittles self, in all kinds of subtle and not so subtle ways.

As a methodology, auto-ethnography privileges voice as it concerns itself with first person accounts of the relationship between autobiography and culture. The students' investigations of leadership developed their voices by placing "I" at the centre of their stories, and their voices became "public" voices by writing their work place narratives. We can discern the practices that develop phonêsis in students: supporting students in telling their stories, encouraging them to read closely and widely, helping them to reflect on how they make meaning of their working lives, demonstrating to them that they can embed their personal stories within a wider socio-cultural context, drawing out and encouraging their creative impulses and persuading them to see the value of the humanities literature in their research.

If we ask what phonêsis looks like in the professional practice of the Wembley students, we could conclude that it is the reflection they achieve as a professional community. A professional community "continually asks and answers, in words and practice, what constitutes 'the good' for each new day and era, and for each new site and situation for practice" (Kemmis 2012, p. 159). I have set out how practitioners enact phronêsis and what they attend to as they reveal their knowledge. As Peter Swordy, the Centre's manager, remarked: "Our objective was to create a climate of trust and loyalty without which Wembley Stadium could not operate safely or effectively. This has been a very important achievement."

Power

In his Reith Lecture "Representations of the Intellectual" (1994, p. 3), Edward Said questions the description of intellectuals: are they "a very large or extremely small and highly selective group of people"? He contrasts Julien Benda's "celebrated" definition of intellectuals as "a tiny band of super-gifted and morally endowed philosopher-kings who constitute the conscience of mankind" (p. 4) with the Italian Marxist, activist and political philosopher Antonio Gramsci's more inclusive proposal that all men are intellectuals but not everyone's "function" is that of an intellectual (p. 3):

> Gramsci's social analysis of the intellectual as a person who fulfils a particular set of functions in the society is much closer to the reality than anything Benda gives us, particularly in the late twentieth century when so many new professions – broadcasters, academic professionals, computer analysts, sports and media lawyers, management consultants, policy experts, government advisers, authors of specialized market reports, and indeed the whole field of modern mass journalism itself – have vindicated Gramsci's vision (p. 7).

Said is referring to the production of knowledge and lamenting the dispiriting absence of the "public intellectual", the "author of a language that tries to speak the truth to power" (p. xiv). However, what he states about this ideal, outspoken and fearless individual, this person who refuses to be reduced, to be a "faceless professional" or someone who refuses "to raise embarrassing questions or to shy away from orthodoxy and dogma" appears to describe closely the best and the brightest students with whom I have worked. None of these students would ever call him or herself an intellectual but many possess the qualities Said believes an intellectual needs to have. The best of these students—from Toshiba, Wembley and we will see from the Halifax—exhibit the heart of Said's intellectual:

> The intellectual's representations, his or her articulations of a cause or idea to society, are not meant primarily to fortify ego or celebrate status. Nor are they principally intended for service within powerful bureaucracies and generous employers. Intellectual representations are the activity itself, dependent on a kind of consciousness that is sceptical, engaged, unremittingly devoted to rational investigation and moral judgment [...] Knowing how to use language well and knowing when to intervene in language are two essential features of intellectual action (p. 15).

I recognise that Said is depicting an intellectual, an academic detached from the university or company or state, a disinterested individual who comments from the margins of society. These students work for "generous employers", employers willing to expose their flaws because they trust that their employees—many of whom are passionate and committed—will provide the valuable insight into how the former can improve how they function through the benefit of the latter's innate wisdom.

Antonio Gramsci

I want to turn briefly to Antonio Gramsci's notebooks (*Quaderni del carcere*) written by him in prison between 1929 and 1935. Gramsci's interests range from ideas on civil society, the nation-state and cultural hegemony which appear to designate a phase in which a group "aspires to a position of leadership in the political and social arena" (Gramsci 1971, p. 20). Alliances form around a specific group who then dominate intellectually and morally over other groups. In his opposition to Mussolini and the Fascists and in his fervent belief in revolution against the ruling classes, Gramsci has important points to make which are central to my project of working with students in their organisations. The implications of his idea that "organic" intellectuals who, distinguished from "traditional" professional intellectuals at universities, for example, are those people who can be in any job, relate to my emphasis on the democratic nature of education. Gramsci viewed these "organic" intellectuals as crucial in the role of absorbing ideas "from the more advanced bour-geois intellectual strata [so that] the proletariat can escape from defensive corpora-tism and economism and advance towards hegemony" (Gramsci 1971, p. 133).

I sense a purpose not radically divorced from Gramsci's objectives. Whether or not the students are entirely conscious of their desire for power within their organisations—the power of being able to make decisions to help their careers—they recognise that there is no escape from politics. On their journey of reading and writing critically, of rejecting stale, conventional thinking, and gaining confidence in their own abilities to judge and build on their knowledge, students are not on a mission to overthrow their organisations (in the Gramscian revolutionary sense) but to enhance the mission of their oganisations by developing themselves and their fellow staff. Their power becomes rooted in their new-found expressed knowledge.

I realise how peculiar it appears to try to reconcile an early 20th century Italian revolutionary philosopher's ideas with a work based learning programme centred on students from the kind of institutions he would have urged them to destroy, but in Gramsci's concepts of power, education and intellectual thought, there are parallels to be drawn. For example, let us take his very first sentence, a question, from the *Notebooks*:

> Are intellectuals an autonomous and independent social group, or does every social group have its own particular specialised category of intellectuals? (Gramsci 1971, p. 134)

Gramsci argues that every class has intellectuals, but if we go beyond the concept of "class" and focus instead on the idea of noviciates in higher education—non-traditional learners who are receptive to innovative ideas and indeed revolutionary ways of looking at organisational problems—his ideas have currency within the work based learning curriculum. My concern is not with revolution but with improving workplace learning by teaching literature and, at this juncture, the philosophers who can illuminate the crucial role critical thinking and the raising of a strong and maybe dissenting voice can have on learning. Said's (1994, p. 17) description of what real intellectuals should be thinking and doing is similar to what we should be engendering in our students:

> the intellectual in my sense of the word, is neither a pacifier nor a consensus builder, but someone whose whole being is staked on a critical sense, a sense of being unwilling to accept easy formulas, or ready-made clichés, or the smooth, ever-so-accommodating confirmations of what the powerful or conventional have to say and what they do. Not just passively unwilling, but actively unwilling to say so in public.

Perhaps my project is in producing revolutionaries after all. Although not revolutionaries in the sense of overthrowing institutions and state, but those willing to continually interrogate those institutions while challenging themselves to become thoughtfully critical for the benefit of their companies. Naturally in Marxist ideology such a way of thinking and behaving would be absurd, but for work based learning students, it is a healthy and productive way of participating in a democracy.

Gramsci acknowledged the hegemonic power of rhetoric, of being able to use language with precision and cogency. His focus was on creating intellectuals from the working class and his perspective was a revolutionary one. He does, however, have much to say that we can learn from today. He views specialised schools with precise boundaries as institutions apart from "humanistic" schools which are "designed to develop in each human being an as yet undifferentiated general culture, the fundamental power to think and ability to find one's way in life" (p. 165). He deplored the tendency to develop specialised schools, useful, mechanical education and methodical and task orientated learning. The ideal learning took place:

> through a spontaneous and autonomous effort of the pupil, with the teacher only exercising a function of friendly guide – as happens or should happen in the university. To discover a truth oneself, without external suggestions or assistance, is to create – even if the truth is an old one. It demonstrates a mastery of the method, and indicates that in any case one has entered the phase of intellectual maturity in which one may discover new truths (p.175).

Conclusion

The ability to question matters critically is essential for democracy as the more contemporary philosopher Nussbaum (2010) contends. In business it makes sense to question authority and to strengthen one's skills of independent thinking. Nussbaum (2010) considers some of the biggest corporate disasters in the United States—the failures of Enron and WorldCom, for example—occurred because of a culture of complacency where critical voices were not articulated. The students at Wembley were not hired because they were security experts. They were not hired nor do they continue to excel because of any kind of narrow specialisation but because of their commitment to thinking creatively. Carrie discusses the importance of trust as an ethical dimension of leadership as she relates a recent incident:

During a busy music concert this summer customers were not happy with the seating line or the sound quality. Crowds began to form at the customer service information booth and it got to be quite overwhelming as staff were finding it hard to control the customers. I identified a particular member of the team and suggested he take on a temporary team leader role and help to manage and disperse the crowd. He did a very good job and organised the customers so that they eventually all dispersed.

Staff often feel ill equipped to take on leadership roles, but I think, as a manager, I need to step back and allow staff to develop. Everyone likes their moment of recognition and by empowering them to achieve it, it also inspires those around them to step up and lead. It's really about winning trust to enable people to learn and develop their ideas and strategies.

The moral issue of trust should to be at the heart of any professionalised activity. Instead of doing what she was supposed to do—handle a situation and instruct one's team members accordingly as the organisation expected—Carrie decided to trust a team member to handle the situation in a leadership role. Ultimately what I have been delineating is a way of mobilising reflective learning and a more questioning approach in organisations through using literature, especially in the humanities.

Nussbaum (2010) views the marginalisation of the humanities as deeply damaging for the future of democracy. I intend to demonstrate that my work with Wembley Stadium and the Halifax, which I detail in the next chapter, could be used as blueprints for universities to work with corporate business. Nussbaum makes the connection between the economic privileging of more technical subjects with the side-lining of the humanities with the end result an erosion of democracy. Work based learning can play a part in turning this anti-democratic tide. From my experience in higher education as well as from my own reading, I recognise Nussbaum's concerns as legitimate: the humanities have less and less influence educationally year after year. Yet there is an open door through which we can introduce aspects of a liberal arts curriculum and it is an open door through which receptive, mature and willing students who have not had the chance to access literature can finally do so. This is an opportunity many teachers and lecturers never get and we in work based learning must capitalise on it.

References

Aristotle, (2009). *The Nicomachean Ethics*. Translated by David Ross. Oxford: Oxford University Press.

Bacon, F. (1983). In J. Pritcher (Ed.). *The Essays*. London: Penguin.

Barnett, R. (2007). *A Will to Learn*. Oxford: Oxford University Press.

Bass, B., & Steidlmeier, P. (2004). Ethics, Character, and Authentic Transformational Leadership. In J. Ciulla (Ed.), *Ethics, The Heart of Leadership (second edition)*. Westport and London: Praeger.

Bennis, W. (1989). *On Becoming a Leader*. Reading, MA: Addison-Wesley.

Bolden, R., & Gosling, J. (2006). Leadership Competencies: time to change the tune? *Leadership, 2*(2), 147–163.

Brennan, L. (2003). *Integrating Work Based Learning into Higher Education*. UVAC.

Ciulla, J. (Ed.). (2004). *Ethics, The Heart of Leadership* (second edition).Westport and London: Praeger.

Collini, S. (2011). From Robbins to McKinsey. *London Review of Books.* 33(16), 9–14.

Connor, H. (2005). *Work Based Learning into Higher Education.* UVAC.

Docherty, T. (2011). *For the University: Democracy and the Future of the Institution.* London: Bloomsbury Academic.

Eliot, G. (1991). George. In J. Gross (Ed.), *The Oxford Book of Essays.* Oxford: Oxford University Press.

Ellis, C. & Bochner, A. P. (2000). Autoethnography, personal narrative, reflexivity: researcher as subject. In N. K. Denzin & Y. S. Lincoln (Eds.). *Handbook of Qualitative Research* .Thousand Oaks, CA: Sage.

Gibbs, P. (2011). *Heidegger's Contribution to the Understanding of Workbased Studies.* Dortrecht: Springer.

Gramsci, A. (1971). In Q. Hoare & G. N. Smith (Eds.). *Prison Notebooks.* London: Wishart.

Kemmis, S. (2012). Phronêsis, experience and the primacy of praxis. *Phronêsis as professional knowledge: Practical wisdom in the professions* (pp. 147–162). Rotterdam: Sense.

King, M. (2007). *Workforce development: how much engagement do employers have with Higher Education?* Council for Industry and Higher Education.

Kinsella, E. A., & Pitman, A. (Eds.). (2012). *Phronêsis as Professional Knowledge: Practical Wisdom in the Professions.* Rotterdam: Sense.

Nussbaum, M. (2010). *Not For Profit: Why Democracy Needs the Humanities.* Princeton and Oxford: Princeton University Press.

Readings, B. (1996). *The University in Ruins.* Cambridge, MA: Harvard University Press.

Raelin, J. (2007). Toward an Epistemology of Practice. *The Academy of Management Learning and Education, 6*(4), 495–519.

Said, E. (1994). *Representations of the Intellectual* (Reith Lectures). London: Vintage.

Solomon, R. (2004). Ethical Leadership, Emotions, and Trust: Beyond 'Charisma'. In J. Ciulla (Ed.), *Ethics, The Heart of Leadership (second edition).* Westport and London: Praeger.

Sternberg, R. J., & Lubart, T. I. (1995). *Defying the Crowd. Cultivating Creativity in a Culture of Conformity.* New York: The Free Press.

Tate, W. (2012). "Managing Leadership from a Systemic Perspective". *Centre for Progressive Leadership. White Paper, 1,* 1–31.

Waterhouse, J. (2007). From Narratives to Portraits: methodology and methods to portray leadership. *The Curriculum Journal., 18*(3), 271–286.

Wembley National Stadium. (n.d.). *The Organisation: Courses.* Retrieved from http://www.wembleystadium.com/Organisation/Courses.

Chapter 4
Halifax: The Cornerstone of Learning

Abstract When I suggested to Halifax students that broadening their reading would strengthen their educational experience, I had not explicitly suggested George Orwell's works, particularly his harrowing story of a dystopian universe in which there is imprisonment without trial, public executions, constant state interference and the total suppression of human freedom. I drew no parallel between the brutal totalitarianism of a faceless, centralised state and the UK's largest provider of mortgages and savings accounts, as well as one of the UK's largest community investors. Yet students examined *Nineteen Eighty-Four* as well as Alan Sillitoe's *Saturday Night, Sunday Morning* and Niall Ferguson's *The House of Rothschild* to explore the inevitable tensions between life and work. The Halifax students saw themselves as far more than problem-solving technicians: their learning helped them to see their lives and work in a completely fresh way. They were able to use their reading to understand their fellow human beings and to better understand the human condition. In the words of one of the students, "I would definitely recommend other companies [to invest in a programme like this] because it makes colleagues feel more rewarded and loyal towards their employer."

If you went through life refusing all the bait dangled in front of you, that would be no life at all. No changes would be made and you would have nothing to fight against. Life would be dull as ditchwater.

All I'm out for is a good time – all the rest is propaganda.

– Alan Sillitoe, *Saturday Night, Sunday Morning*

Banking consists essentially of facilitating the movement of money from Point A, where it is, to Point B, where it is needed.

– 3rd Lord Rothschild

© The Author(s) 2016

C.A. Eastman, *Improving Workplace Learning by Teaching Literature*,
SpringerBriefs in Education, DOI 10.1007/978-3-319-29028-7_4

Introduction

I would like to begin this discussion with an excerpt from an interview I conducted with a Halifax student in late 2014. The excerpt offers an invaluable insight into perceptions of the corporate world and introduces a number of themes to which I will return throughout this chapter:

> I would say I was fairly immersed in corporate culture up until the banking crisis when I became disillusioned about banking and the corporate world. I became incredibly cynical about the internal workings of banks in general. I think in the corporate world people are fed messages, most of them not relevant. I look at a lot of corporate advertising campaigns and I'm a bit cynical about them too. Although I do think, where customers are concerned, most companies, particularly my company, have been forced to be more transparent about what they are doing, why they are doing it and what the costs are to the customers. I started to read *Nineteen Eighty-Four* and saw parallels between it and corporate life. There is the official perception – things being fed through the system as undeniable, unshakable facts – something I identify with corporate life. There are people who are good workers, loyal to their companies – I really don't want to read too much into it – but like in *Nineteen Eighty-Four* they are being kept under control. There seems to be a lot of manipulation.

When I suggested to Halifax students that broadening their reading would strengthen their educational experience, I had not explicitly suggested George Orwell's works, particularly his harrowing story of a dystopian universe in which there is imprisonment without trial, public executions, constant state interference and the total suppression of human freedom. I drew no parallel between the brutal totalitarianism of a faceless, centralised state and the UK's largest provider of mortgages and savings accounts, as well as one of the UK's largest community investors (Industry News 2012). This student's testimonial illustrates two major points: first, it is clear that the Halifax has changed for the better since the financial crisis of 2008; second, the less than flattering remarks made by this student indicate paradoxically that the company is investing in its staff by enabling its employees to think critically about current practice and suggest ways the Bank can improve.

In this chapter, I intend to demonstrate that the Halifax is investing in the cognitive development of its workforce; it is at the forefront of professional education in the UK with its innovative approach to management challenges. Furthermore, Orwell's *Nineteen Eighty-Four*, with its catchwords used universally as a scourge to condemn the kind of institutional practices inherent in a totalitarian regime, invokes a world that is the very antithesis of this confident, open, progressive organisation. I will return to what this student has said, putting her words about *Nineteen Eighty-Four* into the larger context of the literature the students read, how they used it and why literature is such a fundamental aspect of workplace learning.

Background and Context

Since the end of 2010, over 300 undergraduates have completed the Advanced Diploma in Retail Banking Practice, a course offered by the Institute for Work Based Learning in conjunction with Halifax. The students complete the first two stages of their Middlesex University accredited course at their branches and then embark on stage three which is delivered at Middlesex University over two days with on-going web-based tutorial support. These three stages are called the Journey in Practice. In order to achieve the diploma at the end of the four month course, the students must complete a 1500 word summary of the key issues affecting both their branches and the business as a whole, a 4000 word business plan identifying problems and finding innovative solutions to them again both at branch level and for the business and a final 500 word reflective piece. Each cohort comprises between 45 and 60 students and January 2015 saw my thirteenth cohort of students after four years' experience of teaching on the programme. During the two full days of seminars held on the University campus the students learn how to cite and reference, find articles on the library website and begin to understand precisely what is expected of them in terms of their assessments (the three pieces of work I outlined). During these seminars, I outline my expectations to the students in terms of their on-line participation. The seminars on campus are reinforced by the students' engagement on the VLE: they exchange ideas, suggest reading and critique each other's drafts.

Before I even meet the students for the first time, many of them have already posted their comments on-line about what they expect to achieve from their diploma course. The following should provide an idea of both the students' personal desires and Halifax's requirements:

> I've been working for the Halifax for 29 years. Now it's time to stretch myself and embark on an academic career.

> For the past two years my results have been good but I am looking for new ways to improve the customer experience.

> Our service levels have improved over the past six months but I am still concerned with how colleagues react to coaching.

> Through this qualification what I hope to gain is to look at things from the bigger picture and have a wider knowledge of what impacts my branch.

> I want to understand the key challenges affecting my business.

Since students know that they will be investigating how to address branch problems, they come into the classroom on the first day with a range of questions they want to investigate–whether the commonly accepted NET promoter score is an accurate way of measuring service, whether presenteeism is just as corrosive as absenteeism, which internal and external factors contribute to business success or failure. I recognise that students require clear and explicit direction on how to translate their ideas, experiences and research into resolving work based problems. My objective is then to support them to develop themselves, as well as help them to bring clarity to their working lives. There are some specific tasks I am expected to do with the students: PEST and SWOT analyses, for example. There are also some specific tasks they are expected to undertake: a competitor overview, a review of transacting customers, a reflection on the key themes on leading and implementing change. The goal of the Halifax course as a whole is to implement, embed and build on the Journey in Practice solutions so that the students' performance and the performance of their branches are improved. The intention is that through the final stage of an academic undertaking, the students will be able to consolidate their learning from the in-house activities and coaching in order to become more effective members of their organisation.

Literature and Liberty

There is a multitude of ways in which being a member of an organisation can manifest itself: perhaps as though on a spectrum—on one end, an autonomous free thinker, on the other end, a *Nineteen Eighty-Four* definition of the worker as a brainwashed automaton. Orwell may appear at first sight to be a strange choice of author for students working in a bank. Orwell, of course, was no proponent of capitalism, and banks are at the core of how a capitalist society functions. He had fiercely attacked capitalist society in *Down and Out in Paris and London* (1933) and in *The Road to Wigan Pier* (1937) (Eckstein 1985). Specifically, in 1949, when he thought *Nineteen Eighty-Four* was being used by the American Republicans to satirise the British Labour Party he wrote:

> My recent novel is *not* intended as an attack on Socialism or on the British Labour Party (of which I am a supporter) but as a show up of the perversions to which a centralized economy is liable and which has already been partly realised in Communism and Fascism. I do not believe that the kind of society I describe necessarily *will* arrive, but I believe (allowing of course for the fact that the book is a satire) that something resembling it could arrive. I believe also that totalitarian ideas have taken root in the minds of intellectuals everywhere, and I have tried to draw these ideas out to their logical conclusion. The scene is laid in Britain in order to emphasize that the English-speaking races are not innately better than anyone else and that totalitarianism *if not fought against*, could triumph anywhere (Eckstein 1985, p 11: emphasis in original).

This chapter will not be enlisting Orwell to delineate the shortcomings of capitalism, but instead will draw on him and the wide range of writers the students read to make the point that literature can provide a rich source of knowledge for students to uncover. Students are keen to articulate their experiences, skills and knowledge as coherently as possible back to their organisations. They want their loyalty recognised by their organisations as well as the permission to influence company direction. The Halifax students want Halifax to have the benefit of their wisdom. When I asked Nick Calvert, the Halifax Journey in Practice Manager, why Halifax decided to embark on an academic collaboration with the University he told me the following:

It was set up by a couple of our senior managers who were looking at our branch managers and thinking – how can we actually improve their professionalism? At Halifax the process for our branch managers was process driven and they miss out on what is happening in the wider marketplace both within the financial services and retail. So, it was really two-fold: first, it was publicly to say we have the first fully qualified branch manager workforce on the high street, in order to re-build the confidence of both customers and colleagues following the financial crisis. However, the equally important objective was actually to up skill our branch managers and give them the opportunity of studying outside of Halifax. Everything before that was internal, so really it was a way of looking to help them to improve their practice by looking at examples in the UK and in the wider world.

Nick Calvert asserts that the collaboration between the Halifax and the University is no vacuous public relations exercise but a solid commitment to getting staff to examine the challenges faced by contemporary business in its quest to effect radical change in banking culture.

Returning to the student who perceived stark parallels between Orwell's *Nineteen Eighty-Four* and the oppressive conformity of corporate life, I have always been surprised at the openness Halifax demonstrates to employee criticism: the company positively welcomes ideas on making corporate life less oppressive. If an employee expresses cynicism regarding the "internal workings of the company", the bank would want to allay these suspicions by initiating a discourse with the disgruntled employee. This is not a company that would attempt to use propaganda to paper over rifts in the workforce. Halifax sees criticism as an opportunity to make itself stronger. In taking responsibility for future professional development of its staff, the company was aware it had to identify internal weaknesses, failures and flaws. I saw my role as drawing out the students' political sensibilities because I recognised how germane they were to any kind of writing they would be doing. I also appreciated how important it was for the students to look deeper than a superficial solution to a problem, something I will discuss at length in a subsequent section of the chapter. Moreover, I perceived that Halifax wanted me to open its employees' eyes: there was never any censorship or a list of proscribed materials. I was at liberty to suggest whatever I thought would be engaging and thought provoking—even something seemingly inimical to the values of a large corporation—because the company really believed in enlisting intellectual freedom in order to promote their strategy and vision. The student speaking about *Nineteen Eighty-Four* acknowledged the value in what her company was doing when I suggested to her that Halifax's engagement with higher education could be interpreted by a cynical on-looker as an empty public relations exercise:

I wasn't forced to do the course, and at the end of it, I really enjoyed the process of putting my thoughts down on paper and feeling I had learnt something about a bigger picture. You go to work every day and look at your emails and you never look at the big picture, so it forced me to do that. I think it's a huge benefit to the company to get people out of the thinking that they normally do.

Orwell did not equate capitalist Britain with a fascist state nor did he believe that any entity had the right to exploit others for profit (Eckstein 1985, p. 15). Our minds naturally associate banks with profit making, yet ironically Halifax is a financial institution that is promoting wholesale intellectual freedom. That intellectual freedom comprises "looking at the bigger picture" wherever possible. Orwell's excoriating views on totalitarianism were rooted in what he saw of the social conditions of the modern world, of a dispirited condition of people. He detested capitalism but he was willing "to concede it a crucial virtue" (Eckstein 1985, p. 13). Intellectual freedom deserves to be defended by us all, and I have certainly found that principle alive and flourishing at Halifax.

The Actual Materials

Halifax students are expected to have already completed the first two stages of their Journey in Practice before they undertake their final stage of study at the University. I asked a range of students about their first two stages of the Journey in Practice both informally at the start of our time together and afterwards in interviews and questionnaires. The first two stages urge them to reflect on their learning through coaching sessions as well as elicit their observations on the process of learning through a series of statements. I do not intend to focus at all on these stages because they are not a part of my investigation; however, the statements students make about this process illuminate their attitudes towards learning. During the induction day students generally comment that these stages are "helpful", "useful" and that they "develop skills". On the whole, they are positive about this experience during stages one and two. Of course when the students then progress to the academic part of the course with the University, their work becomes far more analytical and research inflected. What appears to occur is that they start to question "process-related" tasks such as the ones they carry out in stages one and two. The following comments about their experiences during stages one and two encapsulate a common growing dissatisfaction with the "process-related" elements of learning, a dissatisfaction generated by experiencing a contrast between these first two stages and the academic segment of their journey:

> JIP one and two can be really prescriptive and process-driven. The trainers were really, really enthusiastic and extremely impressive but at the end of the day it is just another process. Much of it is a tick box exercise. Your behaviours are observed and ticked off against what you should be doing. It is very easy to become bored with it. I needed something like this [the University study] to open up my thinking.

Donald Schön (1991, p. 331) discusses teaching and the implications for students who are frustrated by the "school as an institution of technical rationality and bureaucratic efficiency". He warns that students will divert their energy and creativity when there are systems of control that leave them oppressed and jaded. I am not suggesting that stages one and two do not allow students the opportunity and freedom to reflect on their practice, but that they resemble an educational bureaucracy as described by Schön (1991, p. 332):

Students learn to evade their supervisors' control, giving nothing more than lip service to the formal system. Such games of control and evasion are often embedded in political networks as individuals form alliances for the purpose of gaining or protecting territory, security, and status.

The stage one and two curriculum is akin to an education bureaucracy in that it is limited to specific themes and skills to be addressed. When the students are free to question the processes rather than simply identify them and demonstrate expert knowledge of them, they move instead toward independent, qualitative judgements that can break the bounds of restrictive, even deadening bureaucracy. As Carly remarked in her interview with me:

[University study] is really enlightening and opens your mind to different opinions. It grows from there because you are investigating a topic which branches off into social and psychological aspects. I felt I was allowed to think differently, to question, not to accept something just because it's the way it's always been done. Every time I see a customer, I always look a bit deeper into that customer. I look at the person and try to advise them around credit and how they can improve their credit rating. We are now trying to get into local schools so that we can educate people in finance at a younger age.

Carly equates the interrogating of authority and the resisting of convention with learning. This is striking because this is not the conception of learning that springs to mind when students reflect on their learning. When I stood before the first cohort back in 2010, I was slightly dispirited by the prescriptive nature of the course. Before me were anxious yet expectant faces and the exciting challenge of providing an innovative learning experience; however, the programme seemed too narrow, too constrained, too conventional.[1] I was even provided with slides that delineated a full day of specified activities. The expectation was to go through each slide—"the benefits of work based learning", "a review of higher level skills", "work to be submitted", "assessment criteria"—and emphasise the key points of each topic, amplifying areas as necessary. There was a slide with research suggestions: "business plans kit for dummies; "businessball.com"; "www.bplans.co.uk". I knew that the students' tasks were centred mainly around investigating their branch and area as well as producing a viable business plan to improve branch performance, and that my responsibility was to ensure that I provided the students with the tools to enable them to do so. Moreover, providing such tools—demonstrating how to reference, for example—needed to be done clearly and sensitively. Referencing, in particular, can flummox many a third year undergraduate, and these novitiates are expected to use and understand the Harvard Referencing System after a day together, a day that is crowded by many other aspects of academic conventions. Above all, the difficulty of meeting the high expectations set for these students is compounded by their intense fear of failure which can be mitigated by the classroom dynamics that I will explain further on in the chapter.

---

[1]The programme had already been devised and set up by Institute colleagues before I started to teach on it. I provide the handbook in the appendix to illuminate my discussion.

Fear of looking foolish, fear of failure—neither of these can be underestimated. These are professional people, people who have been building on their reputations sometimes for decades. They are faced with the unknown in the shape of the mystifying and allegedly "elitist" practices of higher education, and they are understandably dismayed. They have had successes and have acquired reputations and they imagine that not "getting" any of the material will cause acute embarrassment in front of their peers. The fear of failure (doing this "academic thing") following success (carving out a career as a bank manager, sometimes rising through the ranks over a period of years) is actually rooted in the science of statistics. It is an effect called statistical regression toward the mean as Sternberg and Lubart (1995, p. 220) explain:

> Roughly speaking, when a case occurs (such as your highly creative idea) that departs substantially from the mean of a distribution of observations (the average quality of [your] ideas), subsequent cases (your next ideas) are likely, by chance alone, to be closer to the mean of the distribution than was the first observation.

Sternberg and Lubart then give an example of going to a restaurant, finding it outstanding and deciding to go back. People generally find that the food is never as good as the first time, an example of regression towards the mean. In terms of a professional bank manager sitting in a classroom with other professional bank managers, she has a reputation to conserve, perhaps even an exceptionally successful branch she has helped to create: she thinks she has a vested interest in keeping the aura of success she has. If she says something "stupid" or appears to struggle with an obscure concept in front of others, she will depart substantially from the perception that she has built up of herself.

I get everyone to sit in groups of five or six people. Naturally there is safety in numbers: students get to know each other on a informal basis and are able to socialise; they work together on the discussion topics I devise and can "test the water", speaking to each other in the safety of a small group rather than risk exposure and potential humiliation in front of a larger group. There is a small caveat: the attentive teacher must—even in small teams—guard against the phenomenon of group-think which Janis (1972, p. 3) describes as "instances of mindless conformity and collective misjudgement of serious risks". As Janis warns, just because "everyone" seems to perceive things in a certain manner, they are not necessarily right. One must be careful not to acquire an illusion of invulnerability created by group think. For this reason, I tend to avoid asking an appointed (or self-appointed) spokesperson for the opinion of the group, and instead try to elicit ideas from all its members. Nick Calvert shared some light on the negative aspects of group think. When I asked Nick Calvert what senior management felt they were getting out of the programme, he was quite clear:

> [The Diploma programme] has actually widened the scope for bank managers and got them thinking. A lot of people thought they couldn't do it, but when they actually got into the research and reading it got them thinking about different ways they could improve their practice. We have lots of fantastic comments from successful students to say that [the programme] has changed the way they work. It has re-directed their thinking and given them

the confidence to look at other opportunities to conduct their practice. In Halifax, like most large organisations, we tend to be inward looking, focusing on our customers and what we have to offer them. At times, we don't always [get] staff to think for themselves, but [the programme] has given them the confidence to look at the wider world in a different way. Students' conventions were being challenged but they seized the opportunity to think for themselves and to produce business plans which are being implemented within the business.

One of the first articles I use in order to stimulate discussion is Edward Hallowell's "What Brain Science Tells Us About How to Excel" from the *Harvard Business Review*. Hallowell, a child psychologist, details a process he uses for "struggling young people to do better" (2010, p. 123), a process he applies equally well to adults within complex business organisations. I have been using this piece of literature in induction discussions because students find its revelations about job "disconnect" and its more positive side of engagement germane to the difficulties they are having at work. Hallowell's work resonates with that of Schön (1991) whom the students read in order to understand the reflective process of learning. Schön's comments on the crisis in the professions, particularly a crisis of confidence, seem to have specific relevance to banking:

> there has been a disposition to blame the professions for their failures and a loss of faith in professional judgment. There have been strident public calls for external regulation of professional activity, efforts to create public organizations to protest and protect against professionally recommended policies, and appeals to the courts for recourse against professional incompetence (pp. 4–5).

Students relate some of the abuses they are subjected to by members of the public ignorant of the simple distinction between a retail and investment bank manager as they direct their invective for the "banking crisis" at Sheila from the Surbiton branch or Kyle from the Dudley one. What I hear distinctively from students throughout our time together is their discomfort and even hurt from what they perceive as the media led manipulation of public perception which leads some of their customers to group together bank managers who are trying to support their financial decisions with investment bankers who have just trousered hefty bonuses and have little or no dealings with the public.

The Business Plan—A Two-Way Street

> I think more companies should invest in courses like the one we have just taken with you. I really do appreciate the opportunity that was offered to me to complete it – it made me feel very valued as an employee that they were willing to fund such personal development. It has helped me view my role at the bank in a completely different way *by using external reading to learn from in my workplace rather than just be internally influenced*. It has encouraged me to use my reading in problem solving not only at work but in home life too. I would definitely recommend other companies investing their time and money up skilling their workforce like Halifax is doing. *I feel it makes colleagues feel more rewarded and loyal towards their employer* (my italics).

I have quoted my interview with Jane at length because I believe her words contain the kernel of what companies can gain from working with a University. It seems counter-intuitive to think that an external agency such as a management consultancy knows a business or will ever know a business better than the people who have been there and have been engaged with their colleagues over a substantial period of time. From one of the first articles the students read, the findings from a study of 20,000 employees in Europe suggesting a close correlation between illness and even heart attacks and non-engagement with one's manager focus first day discussions intensely (Hallowell 2010). After reading and assessing over 300 business plans, I can safely report that not one has ever advocated the use of management consultants to address any of the problems at the Halifax. As Townsend (1970, p. 95) humorously puts it: "institutional [management consultants] waste time, cost money, demoralize and distract your best people, and don't solve problems. They are people who borrow your watch to tell you what time it is and then walk off with it."

Staff engagement is either the subject of every student's business plan or it is the topic that underpins their plans in some way. Not once has a student advocated the use of an external source to help resolve company issues. As Jane points out, Halifax recognises that its wealth, its expertise, its knowledge all reside in its employees and, instead of turning to any external company for advice, it knows that its banking solutions can be engineered in-house. Staff engagement—through clear, honest and effective communication—is at the heart of an organisation's health (Schön 1991; Sternberg and Lubart 1995; Townsend 1970). Schön considers the case of a company that manufactures scientific instruments. The problem that emerged on the surface was that of production delay, but on closer analysis, Schön ascertained that it was lack of communication between staff. In his words, the successful response to this organisational crisis was "designing a process which will involve the key participants in collective reflection-in-action". He advocates the concept of management as an art, a matter of "skill and wisdom" even "intuitive artistry" (p. 241). On every induction day, I explain Schön's ideas, especially on reflection-in-action and urge students to read his case studies.

Nick Calvert told me that the reason Halifax embarked on the university route for its managers was because "a couple of senior managers were looking at our branch managers and thinking—how can we actually improve their profession-alism?" Through our two-day discussions, the on-line discussions and their final work with the business plans as the centrepiece, I would strongly argue that the following observation from Schön (1991, p. 243) encapsulates what every manager faces within the organisation:

> Managers do reflect-in-action, but they seldom reflect on their reflection-in-action. Hence the crucially important dimension of their art tends to remain private and inaccessible to others. Moreover, because awareness of one's intuitive thinking usually grows out of patience in articulating it to others, managers often have little access to their own reflection-in-action. The resulting mysteriousness of the art of managing has several harmful consequences. It tends to perpetuate the split in the field of management, creating a misleading impression that practitioners must choose between practice based on management science and an essentially mysterious artistry. And it prevents the manager from helping others in

his organization to learn to do what he can do. Since he cannot describe his reflection-in-action, he cannot teach others to do it. If they acquire the capacity for it, they do so by contagion. Yet one of a manager's most important functions is the education of his subordinates.

Schön uses the term the objective "education of his subordinates" to describe the mechanism that Halifax students would recognise as providing deep structural support for clear communication between colleagues. A recent business plan that I assessed "Our Visionary Quandary: can a retail bank with sales targets ever become the best for customers?" does not appear to explore colleague engagement, yet through my own suggested reading and the reading that increased confidence gives them, a thorough engagement with the psychological, social and literary dimensions of communication is, with few exceptions, ever present. Dawn's business plan, which investigates the vexing issue of sales targets, begins by examining brand identity and vision and how customers respond to these seemingly "invisible" concepts. She narrates her own style regarding sales targets:

> Customers have found it refreshing to have their assumptions challenged – when instead of 'hard selling', I thank them for choosing our branch for that day and then explore the reasons for their decision. My presence in the face to face meeting also provides customers with an additional point of contact for future visits, which will hopefully build on the relationship they have developed with my colleagues. [My colleagues'] aim is also to ensure that [customers'] needs have been met during their visit. I feel that a conversation with a colleague which meets a customer's primary need, an explanation of further options where we could make them better off, and finally, an introduction to the manager who thanks them for choosing our business and facilitates an open door offer for our customers who choose to contact us when they need to in the future, are how we are putting customers at the heart of what we do.

Dawn's subsequent use of literature in order to substantiate her interpretation of the company's vision—to put customers at the heart of everything—is what makes her business plan a first-class investigation into the paradoxical nature of selling, in other words, how selling something to the customer becomes a matter in the customer's best interests. She uses a range of reading including Suff and Reilly's (2006) study for the Institute for Employment Studies which argues convincingly, in Dawn's words, that "colleagues who are managed by their inputs and behaviours are likely to take a more long-term perspective which focuses on their own sense of achievement, their personal development, their expertise and their motivation by non-tangible rewards."

Dawn explores the inherent contradictions between being reminded that "service" matters more than sales and the new measurements that cannot avoid volume driven performance elements:

> I wonder whether the public face of the vision is different from the messages being communicated internally. Externally the aim of the vision is to change public perception of the Halifax from a bank that miss sold payment protection insurance and had huge bonuses driving dysfunctional behaviours. The vision aims to re-brand the Halifax as a bank that has abolished incentive schemes and introduced a 'balanced scorecard' to ensure colleagues are motivated by customer service, people development, risk management and sales.

She enlists the research of Edelman (2010) and Farr (2009), in particular, to make the compelling argument that removing bonuses deals only with the symptom of compromising organisational integrity: the root of the problem is sales culture, and that colleagues' performances need to be measured through a partnership with their managers. Such a bond would foster cooperation between the manager and her staff as well as foster a relationship based on trust, empowerment and engagement. What is particularly exciting about Dawn's research is that she has found a research subject—the impact of the removal of sales targets on business—that has remained relatively unexplored. Through her own reading she has been able to build a substantiated case that the lack of trust in retail banks cannot be repaired by fashioning a "vision". The vision can be a basis on which to establish and rebuild public trust, but, drawing on Edelman, she argues that the public has valid reasons to be cynical about corporate visions. Her action plan includes the very sensible aim of observing her colleagues to gauge their skills when discussing customer finance. Her objective, then, is to engender efficient and clear communication throughout her branch, and the questions she poses and the story she tells are substantiated by a thorough engagement with literature related to business studies.

Another business plan with an entirely different feel yet with effective communication at its core was Adam's. He used a range of literature from psychology and nursing – the *British Journal of Educational Psychology*, *Royal College of Nursing Great Britain* and the *Journal of Applied Psychology* to make the point that a strong, corporate culture should acknowledge and appreciate employees' hard work, particularly when exceptional performance is delivered and achieved. Drawing on research within nursing education, Adam was able to argue persuasively that good colleague engagement and coherent communication were crucial elements in creating a positive mental state of mind as well as the ingredients in producing a sense of significant persistence in people when faced with difficulties. I was especially pleased by the focus on written communication:

> New procedures and processes are first of all communicated via a branch update; this is then interpreted by the reader and put into place by the branch. If communications are misinterpreted then this could expose the company particularly if procedures were not correctly implemented. Buday and Theil (2013) argue that bad writing actually costs a company as well as doing irreparable damage. An example of this concerns the production of a new guide detailing the information about types of withdrawals. There were sections which could have been open to misinterpretation. This is a clear case of operational risk which, if not managed the right way, has serious consequences for any organisation.

Writing well is such an important aspect of communication that an organisation is prudent to promote it. As I mentioned earlier, helping students to analyse text in fine detail—guiding them to pick out key words, imagery and points of view—is crucial. In fact, during our second seminar (which is generally about six weeks after the first), I provide a truncated version of my Effective Writing module in which I select a text and then ask them, in groups, to provide the following analysis:

- What is the author's authority?
- What is the purpose of the text?

- Who is its audience?
- Whose interests are being served by publishing the text?
- Does the author maintain neutrality in his choice of words?
- Is the writing biased in any way?
- Does the author accomplish his objective?

The exercise is designed to promote the concept of critical reading in which students attempt to decode the academic text. I see one of my main roles in teaching as attempting to dissuade students from reading in a mechanical, passive manner and instead to remain as alert as possible to the purposes of the text. Derek Attridge (2004, p. 82) reminds us that people inhabit an "idioculture, the deposit of our personal history as a participant in a number of ill-defined and often conflicting cultural fields" and for this reason we must continuously subject our assumptions to the strongest scrutiny. The students on the Halifax programme, like any other members of staff in a large organisation, can become acculturated to accept corporate messages without scrutinising them—like many, their institutionalisation can result in a lack of critical engagement with everyday messages and missives.

Babbitt Saves Banking: A Discussion on Literature

A quick survey of business plan themes from one term offers an insight into the areas investigated by Halifax students:

- Designing processes that offer more help to customers in terms of mortgage protection
- Improving customer service by raising skills levels in branches
- Providing an ethical solution to payday loans
- Getting the company recruitment process right
- Reflecting on how the Halifax can educate UK students in finance
- Getting colleagues to perform at optimum levels through coaching
- Addressing change by analysing management styles
- Improving team motivation
- Growing public trust and confidence in the Halifax

One would expect that business plans in this area would focus predominantly on finance and economics based literature. However, a survey of works cited by students solely from one term reveals a high preponderance of articles exploring issues in banking and finance from more philosophical, psychological, historical and literary platforms, providing real interdisciplinary rigour: some of the following titles and authors struck me as exemplary of a solid interdisciplinary investigation:

- Stiglitz on values and ethics in the *Journal of Change Management*
- Carnegie on winning friends and influencing people
- An examination of Archbishop of Canterbury Justin Welby's speech on payday loans

- An examination of Aneurin Bevin's 1959 speech to the Labour Party
- An in-depth investigation into the history of Taylorism in the UK
- Albert Schweizer's thoughts on success and happiness
- Charles Darwin's ideas on evolution from the *Origin of Species*
- Alain de Botton on the *Consolations of Philosophy*

This chapter might have been entitled "How Babbitt Saved Banking". I had contemplated asking the Halifax students to read Sinclair Lewis' Nobel prize-winning novel *Babbitt* because I thought that Lewis' preoccupations with the pressures and values of corporate life would provide them with a perspective through which to view their own experience at work. Lewis focused on the ways men and women might live and work in an American landscape as well as on the moral and political implications of how they communicate. The author's early novels and stories were among the first to examine the emerging "bureaucratic organization of modern society and the conformity of middle-class social life" (Augspurger 2001, p. 76). Moreover, since so many of the students discussed and wrote about the idea of oppressive corporate mind sets, I concluded that Lewis has a great deal to say to the modern reader about being trapped in a strait jacket of mechanised and socialised conformity. Because the Halifax students used expressions such as "thinking outside the box", "wanting the confidence to achieve", "wanting to influence the business in positive ways", I thought that reading about George Babbitt's transformation from a prosperous property dealer to a zestless man uncertain of the formal and fixed certainties of his life would have transformative lessons for the students in their examination of the limitations and constraints of corporate life. I am confident that *Babbitt* would have had much to say to the Halifax students. But the novel's potential for enlightening their reflection on work remained, in the end, only a distant possibility.

I did have the opportunity to see how *Babbitt* could transform the learning of other students. I asked students who were doing post-graduate coaching degrees (I will discuss this in the final chapter) to read Sinclair Lewis' novel *Babbitt* because I thought the eponymous character's journey would resonate with them particularly in terms of the search for a "true self" which appears to be a centralising theme in coaching. The idea of a "true self" is germane to the novel as Babbitt starts to question his existence. Because I have a postgraduate student sometimes for a year or more, we are able to build up a relationship via Skype. Asking the Halifax students to read and discuss a 400 page novel in addition to producing their summaries, business plans and reflective statements seemed far more of a leviathan task than for the student who has far more ample time if only because of the length of time for his or her postgraduate project.

The time I have with each Halifax cohort is limited. Because of these time constraints as well as the realisation that undertaking a literary enterprise such as reading *Babbitt* could be overwhelming, I persuaded the students to focus on two journal articles—Edward Hallowell's "What Brain Science Tells Us About How to Excel" and John Hendry's "Educating Managers for Post-Bureaucracy: The Role of the Humanities". I chose Hallowell's article because it is an engaging story that explores the psychological challenges of matching individuals to job roles and Hendry's because, although a more difficult read in terms of content and vocabulary, it presents a thorough discussion on the types of concerns that surface again and again from Halifax students. Students find that many of the questions that emerge from Hendry's investigation of twenty-first century management issues are those that have been bubbling under their consciousness for years: they welcome the opportunity to discuss the themes with which Hendry engages. From the article I put to them five questions for discussion:

- Do we live under a tyranny of economics?
- What should the role of education be?
- Are personal, social and self-development less important than financial gain?
- Is trust the cornerstone of a healthy organisation?
- How can the humanities contribute to the development of a new managerial identity?

These questions more often than not mould their business plans and will have an eventual effect not only on their branch but also on the business as a whole. Hendry's warning that we are all damaged by the tyranny of economics has a profound effect on many of the students:

> The exercise of power by multinational corporations [is hard] to challenge politically, but it [...] is visible and contested. Moreover, while the managers of these corporations may sometimes, like their counterparts in government, be lacking in the capacity for moral engagement and in the wisdom necessary for sound judgement, the corporations are not in general the villains they are often made out to be [...] Of far greater concern, since deeper and more insidious, is the intellectual tyranny of the economic mindset (2006, p. 267).

The irony is that, although the students work for a financial institution, they are fully cognisant that "the tyranny" of economics has its toxic tentacles all over society, particularly within the poor and disenfranchised communities in which many of their branches may be located or serve as part of a wider area. Some of the most memorable business plans I have read have addressed the creeping prevalence of payday loans and their deleterious effect on the communities in which the students believe their branches should play an important part. Here is a sample of recent excerpts on this topic. Evident is the comprehension that responsible finance is integral to a healthy, functioning society, not an entity apart: responsible finance has a clear role to play in community cohesion and societal well-being.

> The research I carried out during the completion of my workbook summary, together with my personal knowledge from within my branch, has highlighted the fact that payday loans are becoming more prevalent among customers. In most cases, the rate of interest charged on these payday loans is significantly higher than a personal loan from a high street bank. I therefore believe that Lloyds Banking Group (LBG)[2] has an ethical responsibility to address this problem either by providing an equivalent but cheaper product that suits the needs of a customer who applies for a payday loan or to finance and provide comprehensive education

---

[2]Lloyds Banking Group is the parent company of the Halifax Community Bank.

to improve the financial capability of customers. This will fit with the LBG strategy of "being the best bank for customers" and "helping Britain prosper" (LBG 2012).

The student develops her argument by pointing out that LBG is ignoring an obvious customer need for some form of payday loan. She suggests that there is a strong link between responsible banking and financial stability. She displays an impressive depth of research into the UK digital finance company Wonga (one of the payday loan companies held in disrepute by many social commentators) and offers an impressive analysis of the similarities between these kinds of companies and her own:

> Reports in the press observe that Halifax and Santander have been the main perpetrators in accruing large amounts of money from customers' lack of acuity concerning overdrafts and fees. Customers using an unauthorised overdraft of £ 100 on a Halifax Reward current account would be charged £ 100 equating to an APR of 1200 %. This concerns me and again leads me to believe that consumer education is critical for LBG to be considered the best bank for customers. With HCB, one of the key priorities is to help our customers manage their debt; surely the Bank should offer an alternative solution for a customer experiencing financial hardship, rather than continually allowing them to accrue exorbitant fees. Because an overdraft is a convenient way to borrow money when a customer needs additional funds urgently, he or she will pay high costs to meet these needs. While profitable for the Bank, we never want to go down the same route as payday lenders – those institutions which prey on the vulnerable.

It is important that students see through corporate rhetoric and do not necessarily dismiss it, but weigh its validity and come up with strategies that make the abstract concrete in ethical and constructive ways. Hendry (2006, p. 268) perceives "contemporary economic conceptions of the role of education" damaging to society and in need of challenging. Nussbaum (2010) makes the point that if economic contingencies continue to overshadow education, the very concepts and principles of democracy are at stake. Her concern is that a society in which the humanities are increasingly marginalised and in which governments emphasise profits before anything else, respect and concern for one's fellow citizens—the cornerstone of democracy—become hostage to the economic growth at all costs argument. The following is Nussbaum's (2010, pp. 91–2) template for the ideal economic curriculum in higher education:

> All students should acquire a solid understanding of the basic principles of economics and the operations of the global economy, building on earlier grounding. The usual introductory economics course is likely to be a bit insular, detaching principles and methods from a study of alternative economic theories and of globalization, but such courses do at least convey mastery of core techniques and principles. They can be usefully supplemented with a course on globalization and human values, taught from the point of view of both history and political theory. At the same time all of the ideas involved in the history studied can be appreciated at a deeper level through a course in theories of social and global justice, taught from the point of view of philosophy and political theory.

The irony is that the Halifax bank managers do have a basic and, in some cases, an extremely sophisticated understanding of the principles of economics and finance and are able to explain how the global economy affects their business. In fact, work based learners, as I have stated throughout this book, are ripe candidates for a humanities curriculum. They truly embody Nussbaum's ideal of "citizens of the world" and are people who are able to perceive that "their own nation is part of a complex inter-locking world" (p. 91). The "earlier grounding" is their job experience and training. Their methods are never detached from their study but instead their study builds on the principles and methods they have been implementing for years. Halifax students already conceive of themselves as members of a heterogeneous society and world. By offering students an interdisciplinary cornucopia of reading in ethics, history, psychology and philosophy, they will absorb and analyse those ideas, synthesising them in order to improve their practice, and, by extension, that of their organisation.

Hendry's concern is that the common good of personal, social and self-development is eclipsed by Mammon: "Artificial measures of economic value have become ends in themselves, driving out less measureable but more meaningful goals of personal and social development and well-being. Economy has replaced humanity as the core value of political discourse" (p. 268).

At the outset of their course, the majority of Halifax students are unaware of the higher educational discourse that privileges subjects that promote economic activity, such as those in IT and engineering and the hard sciences over subjects in the humanities. As Belfiore and Upchurch (2013, p. 1) put it "courses that will facilitate students' access to the job market" are considered of far more economic value than subjects in the humanities. However, because of the nature of the work based curriculum, Halifax students and others can be introduced not only to different literatures that could be considered in the broadest sense of emanating from the humanities, but they are also able to engage via articles such as Hendry's with the critical argument about the value and use of education.

Ethics and Trust

From an informal survey of my last group of students, I discovered that seven out of twenty-five submissions contained substantial engagement with the ethical dimensions of education. The students were able to make convincing cases for financial education programmes for customers as well as for those aimed at schools. They asked questions ethically as well as practically: Is it the responsibility of schools to fill the gap in financial education in the UK? If we are to focus on educating the young for the future, who educates the millions of adults in the UK currently trying to make sense of their own finances? Can education build the trust that has been lost in the banking industry? Much of their writing focused on the concept of trust in banking, something which I contend emerged from exploring a range of literature on ethics, particularly from De Cremer's (2010) research on rebuilding trust. The following excerpt captures Helen's sense of moral urgency:

The need for banks as a retail sector to rebuild the trust that evaporated completely in the banking crisis of 2008 is as urgent as ever in 2014. Customers are still mistrustful of banks as a whole, and the negativity of the media compounds the issue. De Cremer (2010) argues that transparency is not enough, and the banks need to take complete responsibility for their failures. De Cremer points to a survey from 2010 of over 2000 UK adults with 77 % believing strongly that UK banks need to make rebuilding customer trust their central focus. He states that there are three steps the banks need to take to rebuild this trust: communicate change, create a breach with the unrealistic expectations of the past and finally, to make sure any change will succeed, they must demonstrate the principle of 'sacrificing leadership'. De Cremer urges managers to show a vulnerable side, to be self-sacrificing and to put customers before profits.

I would argue that at the beginning of their University diploma course, students have a vague, inchoate idea of ethics, but, by the end of the course, the idea of a moral compass and study with an emphasis on moral education were the core values to which they subscribed. It is not part of my mission to impose any particular set of values on the students – the Halifax Retail Banking Diploma is not an education in values. If we accept the definition of value provided by Burridge and Webb (2007, p. 1) as "the articulation of some fundamental moral principle", value as espoused by the students involves an ineluctable concern for the communities they serve, as well as a justification for the bank's direction.

The concept of trust is the most vaunted value in each student's lexicon. The idea of a "trusted bank" reverberates throughout all of their work. We are subjected to the word that by its over-use is rendered specious and is even regarded suspiciously. George Orwell does not single out "trust" for any special opprobrium, but it could easily slot into a list of words he considers is used in a "dishonest" way: "democracy", "freedom", "patriotic" and "justice" are used by those who have their own "private" definitions and could be considered part of a catalogue "of swindles and perversions" (1946, p. 9). Commenting on the contemporary phenomenon of language tending to "more collective and corporate forms" and recalling Orwell's preoccupation with the passive acceptance of unexamined language, Edward Said (1994, p. 21) makes a trenchant observation about the language we lazily use: "a language community in each society that is dominated by habits of expression already exists, one of whose main functions is to preserve the status quo, and to make certain that things go smoothly unchanged and unchallenged".

In corporate life, as anywhere else indeed, our minds are numbed by a continual supine acceptance of unexamined ideas and language. *Trust*, published 20 years ago, is an extensive examination of "trust" as a concept. Francis Fukuyama (1995, p. 276) delineates his view that economic life underpins all life by examining how culture, history and business organisations relate to trust. If trust implies an ethical base, without trust, fundamental human reactions can harm society. He contemplates late nineteenth century industrialism:

> The United Sates was […] a relatively high trust society throughout the period of its initial industrialization. This is not to say that Americans were uniformly moral or trustworthy. The great industrialists and financiers of the late nineteenth century like Andrew Carnegie, Jay Gould, Andrew Mellon and John D Rockefeller all developed reputations

for ruthlessness and greed. The history of this period is full of scams and swindles and rapacious business activities unconstrained by the dense regulatory environment of the twentieth century. But for the economic system to have worked as well as it did, there had to be a significant element of generalized social trust.

Attending to Fukuyama's final sentence, I do not think there is a theme more relevant to the Halifax student's practice than that of trust and of communicating that trust clearly. Repeatedly, the students return to the idea as one that enriches and nourishes the culture of the team, the branch, the company. Their own in-depth research informs them that healthy teams and organisations are not motivated by self-interest but by social virtues such as cooperativeness and a sense of duty. Their reading of Hendry confirms that the best model of management is one that builds on trust and trustworthiness. Saifur's business plan on the thorny problem of bonuses engages thoughtfully with Hendry's ideas on trust:

A reason why branch colleagues can feel demotivated is the significant change to their bonus structure. The expectations and targets are not reduced but the remuneration package has seemed less significant. Branch colleagues can also feel demotivated by the media/public perception of big bonus culture as the front line colleagues are not the people who receive large bonuses. The media highlight senior management pay and some staff feel disconnected as their pay has been re-structured, often meaning lower performance pay for low level employees. The LBG CES results reflect this feeling as 55 % of staff felt their performances were rewarded favourably (LBG 2013). Some branch colleagues felt that the brunt of the changes in bonuses was taken more by them than by senior executives: the sharp divide between high level management bonuses and the relatively small remunerations received by loyal front line staff could be a contributory factor to these results. But slowly I see that divide being closed. As John Hendry (2006, p. 274) points out, the building up of trust between all layers of employers needs to be at the heart of good management: 'Only if people trust each other will they share their knowledge and insights and so learn from each other, allowing the organization to capture the benefits of their individual enterprise.'

Bonuses do not necessarily motivate people to succeed, and good leadership should remember the pivotal role that "trust" plays in organisations and in all relationships. In numerous accounts of employee motivation, trust becomes the organising motif around which students' discussions on performance, sales, ethics, team-work, leadership and all other topics revolve. Extending the concept of trust to the customer, many students make the link between customer trust and employee productivity, service results and, ultimately, company success. In concluding an investigation into self-service channels, Wendy notes that:

The depth of customer relations is based on customer trust which will then evolve into allowing us to meet more customer needs. These relationships can easily become sour if 'moments of truth' (important interactions that the customer has) are not realised for the customer (Industry News 2012). No matter how expensive or intricate our software is, it is invariably dependent on colleagues using it as a tool for enhancing conversations and instilling trustworthy feelings. People are the key to making any new system or innovation successful. Being enthusiastic, helpful and trustworthy are the prime ingredients in creating solid customer relationships.

The student's identity, especially, his or her managerial identity, is crucial. There have been notable studies using novels to explore organisational behaviour and managerial identity. Czarniawska-Joerges and de Monthoux (1994) edited a collection of essays about nineteenth- and twentieth-century novels they believed could be used in the study of contemporary management practice, given that these works focus on the tensions between business and society. Czarniawksa-Joerges and de Monthoux are correct to assert the benefits of harnessing the power of narrative to the study of business. My contention is that we should get students to read relevant novels to enrich their reading experience as well as allowing them to examine the competing conflicts and tensions between business and society in an imaginative way. Although I had decided against asking the entire cohort to read longer texts such as novels, in 2014 I asked for volunteers among the students to read Alan Sillitoe's *Saturday Night, Sunday Morning* to investigate how literature can teach us how to live, or, more specifically, how to balance the inevitable tensions between life and work. Literature can help us to understand our fellow human beings and provide a platform for understanding the human condition.

Alan Sillitoe's Saturday Night, Sunday Morning and Niall Ferguson's The House of Rothschild: Money's Prophets 1789–1848

Saturday Night, Sunday Morning (1958) is a "working-class" novel that charts a year in the life of an "angry young man". Arthur Seaton works all day in a Nottingham bicycle factory and his weekends are taken up with a colleague's young wife and his first love, alcohol. The novel opens on a Saturday night. Arthur has just polished off seven gins and ten pints of beer, fought with a sailor and fallen down the pub's flight of stairs:

> He was laughing to himself as he rolled down the stairs at the dull bumping going on behind his head and along his spine, as if it were happening miles away, like a vibration on another part of the earth's surface, and he on an earthquake-machine on which it was faintly recorded. This rolling motion was so restful and soporific, in fact, that when he stopped travelling, having arrived at the bottom of the stairs – he kept his eyes closed and went to sleep. It was a pleasant and far-away feeling, and he wanted to stay in exactly the same position for the rest of his life. (Sillitoe 1958, p. 12).

The novel is ostensibly about Arthur's drinking, sexual conquests, fights, fantasies and anger, but in a deeper sense concerns "the pursuit of pleasure and a new consumer passion among the working class" (Daniels and Rycroft 1993, p. 471). As the story of a young urban rebel, *Saturday Night, Sunday Morning* expresses "anxiety about physical, social and cultural containment"—in fact, when the novel gained international success, Nottingham officials accused the author of "stirring up trouble" (p. 476). I chose the novel for the Halifax students to read (I had a half dozen volunteers this term) because it encapsulates the main concerns they have in their retail branches. During the induction, students invariably bring up the problems of payday loan companies and whether or not Halifax should be offering a similar service with a much lower lending rate to their more financially disenfranchised customers. Many are equally vocal about the difficulties of how they are perceived by the public, a perception they believe is mediated by a vindictive media that, in their opinion, encourages the public to conflate retail bank employees with commercial bankers. I asked the volunteer readers to comment on the relationship the characters have with money as well on the tensions between business and society. Students noted that Arthur Seaton's working week was devoted to the pursuit of earning money for clothes and for drinks at the pub. As one student commented:

> Arthur's relationship with money is that it is a useful commodity that supports his lifestyle; he needs it for necessities like his board but it also enables him luxuries such as clothes (his form of investment) and nights out. He is part of the fabric of an "earn and spend" culture as opposed to one where savings are important. However, he does not live outside his means which is a lesson we (and many of our customers) could take note of. He may blow all of his money in the weekly cycle of pay day to pay day, but if he hasn't got it, he doesn't spend it.

My follow-up question was whether the relationship with money depicted in *Saturday Night, Sunday Morning* had any contemporary lessons for the Halifax as a business:

> Characters, in general, don't trust the factory or any institutions representing authority. For example at the factory, it is a game of cat and mouse: rather than working together to exceed production and gain mutual awards, workers and bosses were at opposite ends. We, likewise, need to gain customer trust in order for our business to run well. We could do worse than begin to educate our customers on financial matters in order to mitigate such an atmosphere of distrust. It is clear that "business" in the novel is not considered a friend but more of an entity that is to be vied against. Arthur has worked out how to game the system when it comes to his earnings, and he has little respect for anyone on the factory's (business) side. The factory (or representative business) looms over the surrounding area and we, as readers, never forget its overbearing presence. We, as a business, need to think about how we position ourselves within the communities we serve.

Students who preferred non-fiction to fiction opted to read Ferguson's (1998) *The House of Rothschild: Money's Prophets*, the detailed saga of the remarkable Rothschild family who created a vast, political network, unprecedented economic success and powerful influence over the great statesmen of the 18th and 19th centuries in Europe. Over 400 pages narrate a compelling tale of greed, price-fixing, bribery, intrigue, complex negotiations and savvy dealings on which the fate of Europe balanced, as well as disparaging quotes from the brothers about their customers whom they derided as stupid. In 1835, James and Nathan Rothschild issued a £ 4 million loan for the restored government of Maria II in Portugal. However, since the likelihood of Portugal maintaining interest payment on the bonds was so low, the bonds were "junk bonds" and James regarded those to whom he sold the bonds as foolish:

> We have a great many asses who have been buying this s**t....So the world is now speculating on this s**it. One can gamble with these but one can never hold on to them. (Ferguson 1998, p. 356).

Students were surprised to discern the similarities between some of the Rothschilds' nefarious practices and the more unsavoury side of contemporary banking.
Nichole wrote:

> As the book moves through the generations, the Rothschilds are revealed as philan-
> thropic – supporting art and poetry throughout European society. Yet at the same time
> they were involved in price fixing, double dealing and bribery. There is a great deal of
> discussion about early 19th century risk that is totally relevant today. One of the key
> themes of the book is the development of savings banks created in the 1870s to cater for
> the interests of everyday banking. This move was important in that it was trying to get
> away from banking that was risky which can be related to the increased reliance on
> liquidity of banks post 2008.

She answered for all readers when I asked her what lessons the Halifax could
learn from the Rothschilds' exploits:

> The Rothschilds' influence over governments was partially executed through socialising
> with those in power which seems to be the same way financiers do business. There was and
> still are a select few who rule the country and hold onto the reins of power. Their relationship
> with their clients was fundamental to their rise – I would say, if we leave out their less than
> above board dealings like bribery and price fixing, institutions can learn from the importance
> the Rothschilds placed on mutual support. They were able to weather all storms because of
> their closeness. It isn't that far-fetched to model our colleague engagement on the close
> communication the Rothschilds had with each other and the support they gave to each other.

Nichole has carefully selected one of Ferguson's key points: the reason for the
brothers' success was their unflagging co-operation between the "five houses" that
they nurtured:

> when considered as a whole, the largest bank in the world, while at the same time dispersing
> their financial influence in five major financial centres spread across Europe. This multina-
> tional system was regulated by the partnership agreements which were drawn up and revised
> every few years and which were, in effect, the constitution of a financial federation.

There has not been one business plan that I have read that has omitted the centrality
of branch colleague co-operation, of colleague engagement, of simple "getting
along" in order to reach the goal of business success. I do not think it far-fetched for
modern banking institutions to find helpful lessons from both the phenomenal
economic success and, at the same time, the unethical double dealings of the Rothschild family.

The Reflective Piece: An Opportunity to Tell One's Story, Albeit Briefly

I intend now to consider "culture", what we mean by it and its relationship to professionalism and what it means to be a professional. Within the discussion I will look
at the Halifax students' 500 word reflective pieces and explore ways of re-positioning
them because of their—I would argue—integral role to the course. Barzun (1989,

p. 119), as an educator, focussed on what he perceived as the decline of the humanities and a concomitant rise of specialism in the university as the dominant movements responsible for what he saw as the decline of civilisation:

> We cry aloud for 'communication' and say we suffer from the lack of it. We ought instead to demand conversation which pedants so seldom achieve. For conversation is the principle of good society and the good life. It is the key out of the prison cells of our professions, our vocations, and our hobbies, and no less, of our fine arts and our scholarships.

Barzun's argument is that "culture", which he takes from Matthew Arnold's original meaning in *Culture and Anarchy* as "the traditional things of the mind and spirit, the interests and abilities acquired by taking thought, in short, the effort that used to be called cultivation—cultivation of the self" is in decline. Barzun states that the term "cultivation" has been bandied about: for anthropologists, the term means modes of belief and behaviour; for sociologists, it means social circumstances; for the cultural industry, it is prestige and money. Yet if we take Barzun's definition from Arnold and examine it through the lens of professional learning, there is much we can learn about the role of reflection in our teaching. Returning to *Babbitt* momentarily, we learn that Sinclair Lewis tapped into "a potent anxiety among the professional managerial class in the twenties" (Augspurger 2001, p. 74). George Babbitt finds himself suffocated by an increasingly corporatised society in which "traditional professional ideals of autonomy, civic responsibility and anti-commercialisation were difficult to practice in an economy increasingly dominated by corporate organization and motivations" (pp. 74–5). The Halifax students' reflective pieces increasingly epitomise the tensions between professional ideals and even idealism, and the conforming and standardising forces of modern bureaucracy. I have selected excerpts from three reflective pieces which I believe crystallise the desire to be a "true professional" and also how to use reflection to, in Barzun's words, break out of "the prison cells of our professions":

> As I near completion of the project, I really see how the University course has helped me to consider the wider banking industry and the political, economic and social implications that affect my business. Schön (1991) best describes how I feel now after completing my work. In his discussion on reflection on action and reflection in action, he sums up how I deal with the day to day running of my business. I use past experiences to plan future events and now *look internally* for answers to any problems I might encounter. The research for my work was simply the starting point for my self-development. (my italics)

> I have become increasingly aware of the role of reflection in every element of my work as a branch manager. I have started to question every element of the business which I manage and therefore can exert effect on. I question whether we are driving the business agenda and focusing on outputs, or concentrating on the customer's agenda and ensuring the best outcomes for them, sometimes to the detriment of particular business metrics. An old proverb strikes a chord with me now that I have looked deeper into what we are doing to become the "Best Bank for Customers". In an article "Less is More" Norton et al. (2007) point out the paradox that the more we become familiar with something, the less we actually like it: familiarity breeds contempt. I would never go as far as to state that I feel contempt for the company; however, I certainly feel a degree of disdain for the fact that management structure and framework can at times seem at odds with the company vision.

To evaluate my experience I would say that it has been productive to research the area of self-service channels and to gain an understanding of why the bank is making this transition. It has also made me question what the bank will look like in years to come and what my job will look like in the future. Something that really struck me was Kohler's (2013) exploration of what jobs would be left after machines take over. I can understand why the bank might go down this road because of customer demand and competition. However, I love my job and working with other people. If I had had more time, I would have liked to research this element of my business in more detail and gain an understanding through reading about what has happened in other companies. I have learned a lot about myself in doing this work and feel that the research I have undertaken will help me step into my role in a more reflective way.

In each narrative, themes of self-development, questioning, reflection and realism are evident: students use this 500 word space to interrogate the idea of professionalism and less obviously professional knowledge. As Schön (1991) argues, there are two competitive schools of thought about managers and management. One view is that the manager is a problem-solving technician. The other is that the manager is a craftsman/woman. Even though the first view has had predominance, managers "have remained persistently aware of important areas of practice which fall outside the bounds of technical rationality" (p. 239). The three excerpts above reveal stories of managers grappling with uncertainty, change and instability. They know that neither their own work nor the work of their organisation can be reduced to technique; they recognise a missing element, an alternative to whatever the prevalent and reigning management orthodoxy is, needs to be identified:

The recent global economic crisis is in many ways a failure at the level of the organisation – where powerful organisations, from corporations to local government became the rogue element in social life. The recent economic crisis revealed the permeability and fragile ecology of even the largest and most rigid organisations (for example, banks) and how the stability of even homogeneous and mechanical administration systems is relative to the perceptions, experiences, intuitions and aspirations of their executive and even junior employees or members(King and Vickery 2013, p. 5).

In their reflective pieces, I discern a touching element of concern for the students' organisation. They identify the weaknesses in the processes and systems of the Halifax and sincerely wish to address them. Through their research, reading and reflection, they discover that the usual safe and traditional methods of addressing organisational challenges are not necessarily the best ones. They especially see that their organisational culture is in a recovery phase, and they are keen to nurture their company through the debilitating effects of a global down turn. As Hendry (2006, p. 275) reminds us a manager is still a human being who has brought to his or her work "unique habits of thought, perception and feeling, grounded in unique life histories."

Providing students with a space in which to reflect is crucial, and I think that limiting the students to 500 words is too constraining. I did, however, conclude from these brief reflective pieces how transformative the students' learning was to them and how much concern they have for their colleagues, and, by extension, Halifax as an organisation. Nick Calvert reported back to me that many students were reading widely now because "they have actually got a bit of thirst for the extra knowledge and they are also more adept at actually implementing what they are writing".

It is clear that the students see themselves as far more than problem solving technicians: they are eager for conversations about how they can best contribute to the "good society", in Barzun's words. They have a keen sense of the relationship between their acquired knowledge and the world, a relationship which lies at the very heart of the reflective process. As I write this, I currently have a new group of 27 bright and capable Halifax students embarking on the Diploma in Retail Banking. I have made some subtle and some not so subtle curriculum changes since my entrée into working with the groups in 2010: I am starting to integrate far more literary literature into their reading and I am far more rigorous about getting them to use a wide range of sources from many disciplines than I was at first. I have realised that the learning that occurs during our time together (and afterwards) is predicated on the qualities that have made these students the good managers they are: Halifax hired them and continues to reward them because they are hardworking, able, resourceful and dependable. In my next case study, I will reveal a group of students who could not be any different from the usual Halifax cohort. My time with them was less than satisfactory, and I hope that by exploring this experience, lessons on learning and teaching will be revealed.

I will allow the student who identified parallels between *1984* and corporate life to have the final word in this chapter:

> I do think more companies like Halifax should invest in courses like the one we have just undertaken [with the University]. I personally found the course very stretching not only from a time point of view but also trying to get my brain back into academic mode having not done this type of work since my college days which were over 10 years ago! I really do appreciate the opportunity that was offered to me to complete it - it made me feel very valued as an employee that they were willing to fund such personal development. It has helped me view my role at the bank in a completely different way by using other external literature to learn from and input into my work place rather than just be internally influenced. It has encouraged me to use research in problem solving not only at work but in home life too. It has also given me the opportunity to graduate which I am extremely looking forward to as I have always believed that I would never have the chance to do so. I would definitely recommend other companies investing their time and money into up-skilling their workforce like the Halifax is doing, as I feel it makes colleagues feel more rewarded and loyal towards their employer.

References

Augspurger, M. (2001) "Sinclair Lewis' Primers for the Professional Managerial Class: 'Babbit', 'Arrowsmith' and 'Dodsworth'. *The Journal of the Midwest. Modern Language* Association. Vol 34. No. 2 pp. 73–97.

Attridge, D. (2004). *The Singularity of Literature*. London: Routledge.

Barzun, J. (1989). *The Culture We Deserve*. Middletown Connecticut: Wesleyan University Press.

Belfiore, E., & Upchurch, A. (Eds.). (2013). *Humanities in the Twenty-first Century. Beyond Utility and Markets*. London: Palgrave Macmillan.

Buday, B. & Theil, B. (2013) "Why Great Writing Matters to Professional Services Firms" The Bloom Group.

Burridge, J., & Webb, J. (2007). "The Values of Common Law Legal Education: Rethinking Rules, Responsibilities, Relationships and Rules in the Law School". 10 *Legal. Ethics, 72*, 73.

Czarniawska-Joerges, B. & de Monthoux, P. G. (Eds.) (1994). *Good Novels, Better Management: Reading Organizational Realities in Fiction*. Churt: Harwood Academic.

Daniels, S., & Rycroft, S. (1993). Mapping the Modern City: Alan Sillitoe's Nottingham Novels. *Transactions of the Institute of British Geographers., 18*(4), 460–480.

De Cremer, D. (2010). Voice: Rebuilding Trust. *Business Strategy Review., 21*(2), 79–80.

Eckstein, A. (1985). 1984 and George Orwell's Other View of Capitalism. *Modern Age., 29*(1), 11–19.

Edelman, R. (2010) Trust Barometer: Executive Summary. *PR Week.*

Farr, A. (2009) Dealing with Bonuses is not the Answer. *Western Mail Newspaper.* 9th September.

Ferguson, N. (1998). *The House of Rothschild: Money's Prophets 1798–1840*. London: Penguin Books.

Fukuyama, F. (1995). *Trust: Human Nature and the Reconstitution of Social Order*. New York: Simon and Schuster.

Hallowell, E. (2010) "What Brain Science Tells Us About How to Excel". *Harvard Business Review.* pp. 123–9.

Hendry, J. (2006). Educating Managers for Post-Bureaucracy: the role of the humanities. *Management Learning., 37*(3), 267–281.

Industry News. (2012). Amscreen Inks Deal with Halifax Banks. *Digital Signage Magazine., 7*(4), 8.

Janis, I. (1972). *Victims of Groupthink*. Boston: Houghton-Mifflin.

King, I., & Vickery, J. (2013). *Experiencing Organisations – New Aesthetic Perspectives*. London: Libri.

Kohler, A. (2013) "What Jobs Will Be Left After the Machines Take Over?" *ABC* 4th December.

Norton, M., Frost, J., & Ariely, D. (2007). Less is More: the lure of ambiguity or why familiarity breeds contempt. *Journal of Personality & Social Psychology., 92*(1), 96–105.

Nussbaum, M. (2010). *Not For Profit: Why Democracy Needs the Humanities*. Princeton and Oxford: Princeton University Press.

Orwell, G. (1946). *Politics and the English Language*. London: Penguin.

Said, E. (1993). *Representations of the Intellectual. The Reith Lecture*. London: Vintage.

Schön, D. (1991). *The Reflective Practitioner. How Professionals Think in Action*. Aldershot, Hants: Ashgate.

Sillitoe, A. (1958). *Saturday Night, Sunday Morning*. London: Grafton Books.

Sternberg, D., & Lubart, T. (1995). *Defying the Crowd. Cultivating Creativity in a Culture of Conformity*. New York: The Free Press.

Townsend, R. (1970). *Up the Organization*. London: Coronet Books.

Chapter 5
Sofra Restaurant Group: The Untold Stories

If you set yourself to it, you can live the same life, rich or poor. You can keep on with your books and your ideas. You just got to say to yourself, 'I'm a free man in here' – he tapped his forehead – 'and you're all right'.

—George Orwell, *Down and Out in Paris and London*

Abstract I was asked to deliver a module on personal and professional development to a group of young, unemployed people selected by the Affinity Sutton Housing Group to work as apprentice chefs for Hüseyin Özer's Turkish restaurant group Sofra in London. This is an account of an educational work collaboration that was unsuccessful, if measured by the usual metrics of success. This chapter illustrates the vital connection between learning and being prepared to learn. The lesson highlighted here in particular is the need to be clear about a student's responsibilities and an employer's expectations. Although the students did not complete the assignments or their apprenticeships, they faithfully kept up their learning journals, an act which leads me to conclude that, if anything, they wanted to tell their stories. I asked Paul, the student who responded to my request for an interview, what was the most memorable part of the course, and he told me poignantly, "the opportunity to tell my story". Some of these students had social and psychological disabilities; others had been refugees. From an academic point of view, the students' "story" could have been much more successful, particularly for such a vulnerable group of people, had I trusted my instincts.

Introduction and Context

In the Spring of 2012, I was asked by the Institute to deliver a module on personal and professional development to a group of young unemployed people selected by the Affinity Sutton Housing Group to work as apprentice chefs for Hüseyin Özer's Turkish restaurant group Sofra in London. The idea was to help the residents of the housing trust to gain employment by working at Sofra and to gain a university

© The Author(s) 2016
C.A. Eastman, *Improving Workplace Learning by Teaching Literature*,
SpringerBriefs in Education, DOI 10.1007/978-3-319-29028-7_5

qualification through the process of reflecting on their practice. There were eight students to begin with—all aged 21–30—and a total of 13 students were eventually enrolled on the course, although a few of the original group dropped out. It struck me that, at least for the students, the primary purpose of the venture, was to learn as much as possible about the restaurant trade—cooking, plating, waiting tables, hosting at the front of house—and that the studying and learning element was of secondary importance. This is an account of an educational work collaboration that was unsuccessful, certainly if measured by the usual metrics of success: students completing their work to a high standard, and reporting their enjoyment in learning as well as experiencing a positive change in their work. From the 13 students who came and went from the course, one student responded to my request for an interview and I will address his responses in the course of the chapter. I also interviewed Alex Mortimer who had been the development manager at Middlesex University at the time and Hüseyin Özer, owner of the Sofra restaurant group, both of whom sat in on some of the classes I conducted at the Covent Garden restaurant.

When I asked Hüseyin Özer what he observed in terms of learning and teaching he said: "They were very fun lessons, amazing. I loved them and [the students] loved them too." I reminded him that not one student submitted any work and he himself had experienced limited success in taking anyone on in any of his restaurants permanently: "That's true. When it comes to work, they are not used to it. It's like going to the gym. The gym can be difficult and heavy, but [if you persist] you cannot stop going and your body wants it. You cannot force people to work. If everything is done for them, why should they bother?"

What Hüseyin Özer is referring to is the connection between learning and being prepared to learn. I have no doubt that the students enjoyed the seminars as well but their enjoyment did not translate to submitting any actual work. In short, they did not have the sufficient preparatory work or indeed academic background to know how to approach an academic assignment. Alex Mortimer, who was responsible for getting the programme off the ground in the first place, provides context to the initiative:

> The idea was to help the students [of the Affinity Sutton Housing Group] to gain employment at Sofra and reflect upon their practice with a view to getting a university qualification. It was all for a good cause – to support people who lacked confidence in the workplace by giving them some experience of learning from a master chef and to learn what it was really like to work in a busy London restaurant.

I reminded Alex that Hüseyin Özer seemed to suggest that the problem with the course was that the students were not used to work, academic or otherwise. Hüseyin Özer contended that the students were caught in a system of benefits that rewarded them for not working. He was adamant that "cheap labour" was at the root of a "vicious" welfare cycle, implying that low wages enticed workers to opt for a life financed by state hand-outs. Because of his own success, he wanted to give back to the community by helping people to learn the restaurant trade. He concluded from his experience with the students from the Affinity Housing Group that, although they were encouraged to do well, the students were not used to work and consequently the initiative failed to take off.

Alex agreed with Hüseyin Özer in this respect: he pointed out that the students "didn't really understand the work ethic". He thought that a future model could have someone "to help them with their own issues and challenges such as confidence boosting". He observed that the students were "really excited" about gaining a university qualification but "found it difficult to adjust to the workplace". Furthermore, the students' previous experience of having little support with and not being particularly confident in school work necessitated "coaching and support" right from the outset of any kind of work placement. Alex thought that there should have been preparatory workshops that focused on "the work ethic", perhaps dedicated to time management, work responsibility and communication skills.

I would argue that, from the business side of the course, what Alex is saying has a great deal of credibility. The programme with Sofra was a pilot project that has enabled the Institute to learn a number of lessons, in particular, the need to be clear about a student's responsibilities and an employer's expectations. Although Hüseyin Özer and I regard the project as having fallen short of its desired outcomes, Alex was pleased to report that Affinity Sutton "loved the project" and deemed it "successful" because it helped residents experience the workplace: some students had two months of work experience to put on their CV; they were able to say that they worked at Sofra. Clearly, everyone involved in supporting the students—the University, Hüseyin Özer, and Affinity Sutton—had their specific goals, but not enough groundwork was done to ensure that these objectives correlated. Now, with sufficient knowledge from this experience, a successful collaboration between all parties can be achieved.

The students did gain useful restaurant and kitchen experience. No one was taken on long-term, staying the course, so to speak, but perhaps Alex's caveat about the necessity of pre-course work is valid. Yet I have discerned from the experience of working with the Sofra students a lack of affinity between their prior academic experience and the demands of the course the Institute had designed for them. I asked Paul, the student who responded to my request for an interview, what was the most memorable part of the course and he told me poignantly, "the opportunity to tell my story". Some of these students had social and psychological disabilities; others had been refugees. From an academic point of view, the students' "story" could have been much more successful, particularly for such a vulnerable group of people, had I trusted my instincts. I needed to have concentrated on the more "literary" side of the course, allowing the students to reveal themselves through narrative rather than focusing on the more prescriptive PEST, SWOT analyses and management style exercises. Although relevant to a student reflecting on her professional practice and development, these exercises are not only irrelevant to a student new to academic work and professional training, but inadequate in capturing the rich and fascinating life stories the students wanted and needed to reveal. Although the students had not completed any of their written assignments, they did, however, keep learning journals, an act that leads me to conclude that, if anything, they wanted to tell their stories.

The Success of Telling Stories

Acclaimed as one of London's and the UK's leading chefs, Hüseyin Özer has built his Sofra brand as the epitome of high quality Turkish cuisine. An internationally renowned chef and food expert, he is also the founder of the philanthropic organisation the Hüseyin Özer Foundation, which is concerned with helping to finance education for children from underprivileged backgrounds (Hüseyin Özer website 2014). He is passionate about food and education, relating to me his story chronicling his own trajectory from an impoverished and illiterate childhood in rural Turkey to the owner of a multi-million pound business. His "story" is important to this story because it is the story of education: "I was dying to go to school so I could read and write and have a life. Education is a licence to live, a licence to work, a licence for happiness. If you have no education you are 1000 years backwards." He is fond of telling his story—a bildungsroman in which he realises the crucial role learning plays in life. The concept of the bildungsroman is an important one in this chapter. A bildungsroman is a novel that deals with the maturation process as it details an innocent who goes out to the world to seek adventure and learns wisdom. It emerges in the 18th century in Germany as a philosophic response to the contemporary novel. "Bildung" is a process in which a character reflects on his inner and outer life and is able to process his experience in order to achieve an individual wholeness (Swales 1978). Although an entrepreneur chef, businessman and philanthropist, Hüseyin Özer sees his primary role as that of a facilitator and guide to the rich treasures of education, and his story is firmly anchored in the bildungsroman tradition. A year after working with the students, I was struck by the fact that I had not made the connection between his passion for telling his story, his bildungsroman, and those tentative steps the students took with their learning journals, which were essentially stories of themselves, stories they needed to tell.

Narrating one's story is paradoxically the undertaking of narrating others' stories: details and themes about the students' parents, step-parents, grandparents, relatives and friends materialised from their own tales, possibly because an autobiography can rarely escape being relational. In fact, Eakin (1999) maintains that autonomy or self-determination in autobiography is a myth: the "first person autobiography is truly plural in its origins and formation" (p. 43). Each of the students I encountered at Sofra had his or her story to tell, a story of the self as well as their relational identity. Paul's journal entries were notable in how he defined himself and his experience in relation to his grandmother: her cooking, the love she had for him, the questions she asked him after a day of work experience—these entries pointed to his attachment to another. Others' journal entries—Ginnifer's relationship with her young daughter, Brian's details about his friends, Lionel's recollection of teachers who had "demonised" him—all were poised to reveal the self bravely and trustingly. All self-hood is relational, an acknowledgement which could have been usefully and sensitively explored. Such eternal questions of identity could have been touched on by approaching the learning relationship through the lens of actual life stories. Halbwachs' pioneering work (1992) on collective memory in the interwar period emphasises that human beings' memory relies on social frameworks around which recollection is articulated. It follows, then, that autobiography has an inescapably social dimension.

No man is an island; no one exists in a vacuum. If I had focussed on these stories, on these relational autobiographies at the expense of a PEST analysis or the analysis of a mission statement, I might have made the connection between relating one's story and being responsible for the next step in one's life. In other words, everyone I spoke to about the pilot programme highlighted the students' lack of work ethic and kept returning to the ideas of responsibility and confidence. What these people seemed to be saying was that the students needed more support to prepare themselves for work, for study, for the combination of the two. They were possibly not mature enough, not self-aware enough, not grown up enough to escape, in Robert Coles' words "the suck of self" (in Ryan and Jenkins 1997, p. 6). In this interview about stories, literature and education, Coles was speaking about children specifically; however, he could have been speaking about anyone who is not sufficiently developed enough to reach beyond her own self-interest and narcissism:

> Indeed one of the greatest challenges for parents is to bring up children in such a way that they're not self-absorbed and full of themselves. I don't see the school psychologist as a big help in dealing with this. This is not what we're equipped to do anyway. We're equipped to understand the human emotions but beyond that is the need for some commitment outside of ourselves. As William Carlos Williams said, 'Outside, outside myself there is a world to explore'. Children need to recognize that world and become committed to it, heart, mind, and soul (Coles in Ryan and Jenkins 1997, p. 6).

Coles' reflection on the difficulties parents face in getting children to look outside of themselves provides an illuminating perspective from which to consider Hüseyin Özer's criticism that society can sometimes "disable" people and can "disincentive" them from wanting to work hard. Hüseyin Özer envisages society as overprotective of its citizens to the extent it has prevented its citizens' self-sufficiency and autonomy. From an educational perspective, Coles' observations on the connection between empathy, to see "outside" oneself and to commit to something other than ourselves have a deep resonance in learning. Paul's recognition of the learning journal as an opportunity to tell his story made me realise how important it was to have emphasised that aspect of all of the students' learning. They all enjoyed telling and writing their stories: this narrative strand should have eclipsed everything else. This was the key to the rest of their educational journey and sadly I missed it.

Sometimes before we read each other's stories, we need to tell our own. Before I could embark on a curriculum of the kind of literature, such as short stories, essays and novels, which can guide us on how to live our lives, let alone less literary work such as academic articles, I needed to allow these students the space to tell their own stories, even at the expense of commencing anything "educational" or "academic". Coles (in Ryan and Jenkins 1997, p. 6) contends that, without a moral education, children will end up:

> like a lot of us here at Harvard and elsewhere who have been brought up in the secular world and who believe in some mix of sociology, psychology and economics. Basically, these are

the three disciplines that we believe in. There are certain brilliant students here – some of whom are even majoring in philosophy – who drive me crazy because they're unwilling to take a stand about anything – other than what they call their own self-interest.

It is not the first time in the history of thought a writer bemoans the cult of self-interest, of narcissism, of moral irresponsibility in society. After World War II, Mumford (1970) deplored the impact of technology and communications on mass culture. He claimed that it was essential to assert one's primacy as a person, not to buy into the idea that machines and technology made all things possible: above all, people needed to desist as much as possible from exalting the power of the self. A decade later, MacIntyre (1981) condemned 20th century fin-de-siècle post-modernist society as one reflecting a distinct lack of morality, observing that an erosion of civility was akin to the 5th and 6th centuries AD of the crumbling Roman Empire. Bauman (1997, p. 77) suggests that we are "victims" of modernity: we are always on the move, forever being pushed and pulled by new frustrations. It is understandable that many of us are motivated by self-interest. The ego appears to be our only refuge in a modern culture that is "schizophrenic", a "tragic" place where one feels at home only with "homelessness".

More recently, Lamarque (2009) offers his own contribution to this debate on morality through a literary lens. In his discussion exploring the connections between literature and truth, he makes the point that there is more to literature than fine writing: fiction can be a tool for teaching outside of its accepted literary context. Through novels we are able to read about how people behave in certain situations and are able to learn truths from fiction. Of course "truth" in a philosophical context is multi-layered and subject to a wide range of interpretations. According to Lamarque, "truth" is "not an appropriate mode of evaluation for literature" (p. 226). The notion of truth does not capture the process by which literature illuminates and provides insight into human lives. Although we can learn truths from literature, the notion of literature as a source of propositional truths does not do justice to the case that literature can change one's outlook on life, and even has the power to instruct: "To come to a moral understanding of a complex real-life situation is not dissimilar to coming to grasp the vision presented in a work of art; in both cases a change of outlook might result" (p. 240).

This change of outlook may encompass an enhancement of empathy. Lamarque contends that empathy is a natural response when attending to fiction: it becomes possible to imagine being a certain person, a state that is surely the antithesis of the condition of self-interest or narcissism. To engage with characters and situations is a learning process not necessarily considered solely to be within literature's domain. We can "engage and educate the emotions" by reading newspaper accounts, watching television, enjoying a film (p. 240). However, the enrichment and enhancement literature provides in "disturbing" the self, in taking us out of our conventional and entrenched ways of thinking cannot be lightly dismissed:

> The phenomenon of the eye-opening effect of reading some works of literature is familiar and can account for the impact of some works on political and social change. Works that vividly bring home the horror of slavery or war or child poverty or capital punishment can,

as clarificationism predicts, have an effect even on people who would otherwise endorse general condemnation of such things (p. 252).

Clarificationism or the idea that certain art and literature can deepen our moral understanding when a message is "clarified" need not imply that a work of art or literature is "useful" or has to "teach" us something, yet any writing that "promotes learning and truth" ought to be valued. Lamarque makes a distinction between works that are overly didactic and try hard to ram home a message and those that advance understanding and may be valued for engendering learning (p. 253).

I had planned at some point to introduce George Orwell's *Down and Out in Paris and London* because, with "simple, direct, undeceived intelligence" (Trilling 1955, p. 150), the author sketches the comic hell of washing dishes in a Parisian kitchen. As Raine (1998) points out, Orwell's style was "rhetorically plain": he is able to say the "unsayable" in honest and straightforward prose: "We are reminded that great art has to articulate fearlessly what it is to be human" (p. 5). I thought that Orwell's story particularly in Paris would allow the students to enter imaginatively his world of fetid filth and abysmal working conditions—the unendurable boredom and lowly serfdom of the humble dishwasher in a Parisian hotel—so that we could open up the discussion to themes of working conditions, testimonials of what it was like working in the past, and depictions of physical poverty that, for the most part, have vanished from the West. Using *Down and Out in Paris and London* could have opened the students' eyes to appreciate that their restaurant experience at Sofra, as well, could be narrated in order to mine commonalities of human experience regarding work. Orwell is one of numerous writers who could have helped the students find their own voices. Works of literature in the picaresque tradition depicting protagonists growing up in poverty and overcoming a series of obstacles would have provided the students with a framework for comprehending their own life experiences and trajectories. Maxim Gorky, Knut Hamsun, Emile Zola, Upton Sinclair and indeed, Charles Dickens: all of these writers could provide something like a model with which the Sofra students could construct their own stories.

Appreciating Stories

Bushe (2000) investigates how best to employ the techniques of appreciative inquiry with teams, and puts forward the idea that sharing stories and "stepping into an appreciative space" is beneficial in developing "a highly effective group" (p. 185). The varied accounts of trainers and educators working with the appreciative inquiry methodology are detailed in Cooperrider's (2000) seminal collection of case studies. Each of these case studies examines the ethical core of the change process in organisations and emphasises the importance of work places imbued with dignity, meaning and community. Each case study is underpinned by an ethos of recognising the potency of positive imagery within every organisation. Appreciative inquiry might have helped my students to articulate some of the barriers impeding their successful integration into Hüseyin Özer's workforce: they might have been able to use this methodology to reflect on the implications, for new staff, of the peremptory and top-down management practices of a highly personalised enterprise and its culture. I am not proposing that appreciative inquiry as a model would have any effect on the rapid turn-over of restaurant personnel in general or that the students would have overly benefitted by investigating issues within a problem-solving frame. I do, however, think that the emphasis within appreciative inquiry on small groups in generating a new and better future by exploring what had occurred in the past could have been usefully employed from the outset of my meeting the students.

After a session I conducted that focused on meeting customer requirements, the students voluntarily read from their journals. No one mentioned the themes that emerged from the customer requirement session. I had explored with them how to define and measure value, what products and services were actually worth to customers, how to build a customer value model. Even though they had animatedly exchanged ideas about what "value" meant to them and they were able to discuss fluently their experiences working in different roles at Sofra, especially the issues regarding customer care, every one of the journal entries related their own stories, their own past, their own expositions of the traditions, customs and habits of their families and friends. Had I attended carefully to this far from subtle message that their own stories, their own pasts, their own identities—for the time being—eclipsed the exigencies of the restaurant and its underpinning professional practice study, perhaps I could have supported them in finishing the course.

Coles (1989) makes the point that there are "consequences" for each of us as we read and respond to a story. The energy of someone's story "invites our own energetic leap into sadness, delight, resentment, frustration" (p. 129). Coles reminds us that psychologists use words such as "empathy" and "identification" to explain our response to other's stories. We may not find any solutions or resolutions by reading stories but we should inevitably find:

> a broadening and even heightening of our struggles – with new protagonists and antagonists introduced, with new sources of concern or apprehension or hope, as one's mental life accommodates itself to a series of arrivals: guests who have a way of staying, but not necessarily staying put (p. 129).

Coles here is discussing his use of fiction to highlight moral hazards to a group of Harvard graduate students, yet teachers can equally use their own students' stories—stories of struggle and troubles, stories of parental abandonment and being unable to find work, stories of living in the challenging environment of a council estate and not having had good, basic education—to instil a sense of group unity and to allow students to develop a more compassionate and imaginative knowledge of each other. Alex was partially right to observe that "we just underestimated the time [the students] needed to get into what they were about to get into." Before the work placements, before the discussions on management and strategy, before the SWOT analyses, we needed to have given the students time and space to reflect on their own lives and the lives of their peers. Yes, we underestimated the time, but we also underestimated the students' own self-perception.

The students were not dysfunctional but they thought they were perceived as dysfunctional. Paul told me afterwards, "I'm not a moron, but they treated me like one." These could be the words of an overly sensitive young person, but I think it is important to focus on them for a moment. The students were perfectly capable of functioning within the restaurant environment, and would have done so, had they been better prepared. As I stated, I am not sufficiently clear on what occurred between the restaurant staff and the students, but I do know that the students needed to achieve a modicum of academic success in order to counter any *expectations* of dysfunction. In other words, I perceived a direct link between their lack of academic achievement and a concomitant accretion of competence, confidence and well being.

In his study into young people experiencing political conflict, Barber (2013) found that the expectation for widespread dysfunction among conflict-affected youth was considerably exaggerated in many empirical studies he had looked at. He posits that youth are more resilient than expected. His concern is primarily with other researchers' definition of "resilience", that they are using the construct of resilience too simplistically and imprecisely. He defines resilience, within a particular application to young people experiencing political conflict, as the quality of someone who can function in the face of risk or adversity in a conflict situation. Although the Sofra students had not been subjected to political conflict and warfare, I think we can extrapolate lessons from Barber's study, notably from his conclusion that "the majority of young people experiencing political conflict appear to function quite competently" (p. 468). The students felt as if they were *perceived* as incompetent and not functioning well. Perhaps not emerging from the chaos of war and conflict, but emerging from broken homes, poor educational attainment and long-term, historical social problems, the students' direct relationship to societal and economic opportunities had been extremely limited. Barber's caution against researchers responding in a universal manner to the functioning of youths caught up in conflict is particularly relevant in the Sofra context:

> No longer expecting a universal response to the rigors of conflict would also acknowledge variability within and between conflicts, and regarding youth themselves, would recognize that their functioning has much to do with the particular ideologies they hold (particularly, if and how they make meaning of the conflict) (p. 468).

If the students felt stigmatised, it could have been because they felt treated as an amorphous group. They did not feel that their individuality was recognised, and their stories were not being given a chance to be heard. These vulnerable young people could have adapted successfully to both the academic and the work demands of the course, but they felt as if they were functioning (or not functioning) as a group: they needed to be treated as individuals in need of understanding and support, but foremost, as potentially capable, competent and self-determining individuals.

Bauman's (1997) study into the challenges of living in a post-modern world makes the point that the psychological effects of living in a state ruled by the realities of mass market consumption and the unbound freedom granted to capital and finance cannot be underestimated. Particularly for people who have experienced redundancies, lack of employment and societal marginalisation, the modern world can be a harsh place. Bauman's following observation of our experience of the world as frightening and uncertain resonates for me as I contemplate how I could have facilitated the learning journey of the students at Sofra:

> In the modern world, notoriously unstable and constant solely in its hostility to everything constant, the temptation to arrest the moment, to bring the perpetual change to a halt, to install an order secure against all further challenges becomes overwhelming and difficult to resist (pp. 11–12).

The students needed a period of contemplation and an appropriate interval so that their peers and I could acknowledge their identity through their stories. Moreover, I neglected to follow a competence-based approach to my classes. Elbow (1986) argues that, although for some teachers, specifying the "ends" or "outcomes" of learning seems counterintuitive, for those who believe in a non-instrumentalist tradition of learning and teaching—learning being for its own sake rather than being about reaching any goals—a competence based approach can be a useful way to shape learning.

It was not difficult for the students and me to listen to the story of how Paul's grandmother's death made him determined to succeed as a chef. She had been an excellent cook, and it was her meals and the love she had taken over these meals that had nurtured Paul throughout his youth. Yet I needed to have made explicit the criteria I wanted to see from him at the outset. For example, had I said, "within two months, I would like you to have compiled your leading journal so that you can then read it back to yourself and comment on how and where it highlights your values", I would have set a reasonable deadline, have provided an "outcome" and ensured that Paul had received the preparation to learn. Providing a do-able goal in a domain that interested the students (writing about their lives) would have offered more structure to their learning and possibly would have ensured more time to then explore the actual course objectives. When I reflect back on the difference between the Sofra course and all of the other programmes with different employers, I recognise first that the students on the Halifax, Toshiba and Wembley courses were already working and, in doing so, were demonstrating the discipline necessary to learn. I had made the learning outcomes explicit for these groups. For the Sofra students, I needed to have gone further: the learning outcomes needed to incorporate the self-evaluation of the learning journals—that self-evaluation as an outcome would have made a practicable and interesting exercise for the students as testified by Paul afterwards:

> I enjoyed writing about myself and my grandmother and thought that the others were interested in what I had to say. I must admit that I wasn't as interested in the academic exercises because sometimes I couldn't see what they had to do with working at Sofra. Because I always wanted to be a chef because of my grandmother, I liked having to look back and remember what made me take that decision. I regret that things didn't work out the way they were supposed to at the restaurant but those things happen. I guess I wasn't ready to take on the responsibility at the time.

Sometimes it is difficult for educators to tailor their teaching accordingly. We find a style, a technique that appears to work and we stick with it. I did not take into account one of the paradoxes of learning that a "beginner must accept much before he can understand anything" (Martin and Ohmann 1963, p. 9). The learning in any academic sense and learning the restaurant skills were predicated on the students' learning about themselves: the students needed to become thoroughly familiar with the world of learning, in this case through stories, before they could traverse more thorny paths.

Motivation and Interest

Since lifelong learning has been considered one of the solutions to the problems of unemployment, it might be useful to explore some of the literature around initiatives designed to address long-term unemployment and, more specifically, motivation. Halsall et al. (1998) undertook a large scale survey (including interviews) of nearly 800 14–25 year olds in either FE colleges or unemployed in a study looking at whether the current places for learning adequately served young people's needs. Their study yielded some not altogether unsurprising findings such as that the majority of respondents valued flexible learning as well as qualifications and, particularly among the unemployed, their perceptions of learning were greatly affected by their previous educational experiences. The authors also highlighted the association of flexible learning with low achievement and stigmatisation.

Brine (1997, p. 103), in a paper concerned with the official policy of the EU in relation to education and training for unemployed people, points out that all too often the unemployed individual is "pathologized" and "blamed for their own lack of confidence, lack of work experience and lack of motivation".

More recently Tiernan and O'Kelly (2014) demonstrated a distinct lack of literature that incorporated the views of the low-skilled and unemployed. This started me thinking about the students' reasons for joining the course. They all had earlier formative experiences in a kitchen that were positive: Paul had helped his grandmother cooking and baking; Ginnifer created cakes with her daughter using a recipe her mother had treasured; Brian had excelled at cooking in school and had worked at his friend's cafe; Lionel felt "at home" in the kitchen and said he could cook "anything". Their motivation for entering into the Sofra initiative was clear. Why then was the drop-out rate so high despite the manifest opportunities on offer at Sofra? For the students, there was a constellation of factors, but it is possible to point to recent research that goes some way in explaining the failure of the Sofra project despite the apparent enthusiasm of the students on the course.

Ahl (2006) posits a different way of looking at the link between employment provision and education and the resulting assumed properties of improved self-esteem, increased confidence and positive growth. The connection between the motivation people need to undertake education and employment in order to achieve such increased confidence and self-growth is more tenuous than we might believe. She claims that educational theories of motivation are largely based on "industrial psychology" and it is taken for granted that "humans have an intrinsic motivation to learn" (p. 393). Classic cognitive, motivation theories from Lewin, McClellan,

Maslow and Herzberg (among others) propagate a misconception of the "adult learner as deficient and inadequate" (p. 386) because the theories conceptualise motivation as an innate essence, a quality that resides in an individual. To these needs-based theorists, motivation is always "latent" and temporarily obstructed by a range of variables such as lack of time, negative school experiences or scheduling problems. The idea is that if most of the barriers to education are removed, motivation will occur. Ahl suggests that instead of trying to figure out what motivation *is*, we should be looking at what it *does*: "If motivation does not exist, or if, at any rate, it is not amenable to new information and does not affect behaviour; it would seem a waste of time and effort to continue theorizing about it" (p. 397).

Maybe people are just not interested and don't value education for itself? In taking a critical stance to the discourse of lifelong learning, Ahl argues many of the theories about motivation are rooted in industrial psychology and have been useful as instruments to control people. Her ideas on trying not to change people, on not viewing individuals as problematic resonate with my experience at Sofra. Perhaps Paul spoke for the rest when I asked him why he left, "It just wasn't for me. I love cooking and I always will, but I wasn't interested in staying there". I wanted the students to continue, Huseyin Ozer wanted the students to continue, Affinity Sutton Housing wanted the students to continue: we were all looking at the question of what motivated them to continue their education. As Ahl points out, motivation needs to be conceptualised differently. They were not uninterested—they simply wanted to do something else. Moreover, as Ahl strongly argues, motivation is about power: had I offered the students from the outset the tools to explore power, the opportunity to tell their stories, we might have had a different outcome.

Wisdom

Meeks and Jeste (2009) conclude that practical wisdom comprises empathy, compassion, altruism, self-reflection, insight and a tolerance for others' values. They understand wisdom neurobiologically as a property of brain functioning, although they concede that the emergence of wisdom from the associated areas remains a mystery to science. The source of wisdom is therefore complex and difficult to unravel. Brain plasticity is an important element of wisdom, and aligned with developing new and successful relationships, underpins what "being wise" means. I admit that I did not capitalise on the opportunity to educate for wisdom with the Sofra students. I needed to have highlighted the "ends" or "outcomes" for learning, to have followed, however loosely, a competence-based approach to their programme of study. More crucially, I needed to have honoured each learner's history of experience, the stories of life's ups and downs, details of familial and relationship challenges so that their wisdom could have emerged.

At the outset of the classes, Hüseyin Özer spoke at length to the students, relating a picaresque journey from early deprivation through hardship, hard work, learning opportunities and some good fortune to the exalted position of a well-respected and financially comfortable restaurateur who was now able to offer those less fortunate a "step up". His tale was long, animated and compelling. He finished with a homily on honesty:

> If you are honest that means you have to work. You have to be proud and have pride. That is my philosophy all the time. With the money I make I help people to study. I created a foundation because I believe helping the community is key.

The students were impressed by his passion for learning. They all wrote in their journals about their own educational experiences, which were disjointed and inconsistent like his. It appeared difficult for them to draw a distinct parallel between formative bad experiences coupled with poor education and a high degree of personal and professional success. Paul even said to me that he thought Hüseyin Özer's story "might have been a bit exaggerated". When I pressed him on why he suspected that, he said, "Just because you work hard that doesn't guarantee success. I've seen this all my life. The system and other people take advantage of you and they take credit."

It was not difficult for me to discern why Paul and some of the others were cynical about hard work. Hüseyin Özer blamed society for the students' lack of work ethic. My suspicion is that the students' experience of learning had never included what I call "preparation to learn". Gagne and others (Gagne et al. 1992) have moulded the "learning to learn" concept, which translates to acquiring the knowledge and skill to learn effectively. Narrativising could have made the students' learning visible to them:

> narrative learning has very strong links to both adult development and transformational learning. As a means of understanding adult development, a narrative framework sees the life course as an unfolding story, one constructed and interpreted by the individual. While the sociocultural-historical context interacts with and to some extent shapes the life course, the meaning of our life experiences constitutes our particular developmental trajectory" (Merriam et al. 2007, pp. 213–214).

Student transformation needed not only to accommodate but also to privilege the stories of these learners: we can all relate to stories on which we can reflect and from which we can learn. The Sofra students had never been supported in their learning, so they did not know what was valuable to learn and what was less so. Chaotic lives and less than effective schooling—which Bauman would blame on modernity and our very existence in a post-modern world—were exacerbated by a lack of self-esteem, a dearth of confidence and a paucity of life choices:

> Socially modernity is about standards, hope and guilt. Standards – beckoning, alluring, or prodding; but always stretching, always a step or two ahead of the pursuers, always forging onward, just a bit quicker than their chasers. And always promising that the morrow will be better than the now. And always keeping the promise fresh and unsullied, since the morrow will be forever a day after. And always mixing the hope of reaching the promised land with the guilt of not walking fast enough. The guilt protects the hope from frustration; the hope sees to it that the guilt never dries up (1997, p. 71).

In such an existence, being given the time and space to learn, to be given a solid preparation in how to learn, how to listen, how to communicate with each other in a mutually appreciative manner, are all of paramount importance. Learning needs to

be handled and addressed differently with people who have not been given the preparation and the luxury of learning. My instincts were right when I decided to persuade
them to keep a journal:

> Using stories to engage students in ideas that are part of course content may be the only way
> to allow understanding to occur. It is also a powerful means of making connections not only
> with ideas but with other learners, perhaps ultimately creating a learning community.
> Whether these stories are generated by students themselves, are case studies, or are fictional
> accounts, they draw us in, they allow us to see from another's perspective (…) we cannot
> assume the rest of the world sees things the way we do. The authenticity and immediacy of
> a story of lived experience takes us into the experience of another. In that way it deepens
> our capacity for taking the perspective of another" (Merriam et al. 2007, pp. 210–211).

What is critical is never assuming "the rest of the world sees things the way we
do". When the students kept their journals, wrote their stories and shared their stories,
they were revealing imprints of their identity. Using the storytelling process is the
first step in ensuring that both teachers and learners recognise that we are all coming
from different perspectives. For many of the Sofra students, this was the first time
they were encouraged to write their identities and to locate who they were in society,
a society experienced as one of anxiety, an uncertain and at times chaotic and form-
less place. In their short lives, they had amassed their own wisdom, a shoring up of
experience against the hardship of life.

Wisdom is borne of experience, experience which can be related through telling
one's story. In their study of how Native American teaching on responsibility can
support Western management perspectives, Verbos and Humphries (2014) make the
point that the "relational ethic" depicted in ancient Native American stories that state
that human beings have the responsibility of acting with wisdom, respect and honesty
with each other is a useful means of teaching management, ethics and strategy in a
business discipline. The authors suggest that we can learn much from the values "that
have sustained communities even in the face of significant challenge and oppression"
(p. 2) and that these values could be used to challenge the principles of business
schools, which "inculcate and perpetuate organizational systems based in economic
theories that create self-fulfilling prophecies of individualistic self-interest and self-
interested maximizing business" (p. 3).

Paul and the others perceived a lack of interest in their stories, in how, up to then,
they had negotiated the challenges of their experiences with their wisdom. It is
undeniable that a busy and successful restaurant business will inevitably privilege
cost-benefit calculations and economic exigencies over a lengthy and perhaps time-
consuming consideration of the needs of potential employees. Because the students
did not conceive of themselves as part of the established restaurant staff, as part of
a circle encompassing those who were experienced and of a "known quality", they
naturally felt marginalised and even silenced. There was no time, or indeed will, to
recognise the students' wisdom. Verbos and Humphries point out that Native Amer-
icans pass wisdom "from generation to generation through stories that become new
with each re-telling" (p. 5).

The pity is their stories did not get a chance to be told. Moreover, they and
I did not stay the course. Wisdom was there, but always just beyond our reach.

References

Ahl, H. (2006). Motivation in adult education: A problem solver or a euphemism for direction and control? *International Journal of Lifelong Education*, 25(4), 385–405.

Barber, B. K. (2013). Annual research review: the experience of youth with political conflict—challenging notions of resilience and encouraging research refinement. *The Journal of Child Psychology and Psychiatry, 55*(4), 461–473.

Bauman, Z. (1997). *Postmodernity and its discontents*. Cambridge: Pollity Press.

Brine, J. (1997). The European Union's discourse of 'equality' and its education and training policy within the post-compulsory sector. *Journal of Education Policy*, 7(2), 137–152.

Bushe, G. (2000). Appreciative inquiry with teams. In D. L. Cooperrider et al (Eds.) *Appreciative inquiry. Rethinking human organization toward a positive change of theory* (pp. 183–194) Champaign: Stipes.

Coles, R. (1989). *The call of stories. Teaching and the moral imagination*. Boston: Houghton-Mifflin.

Cooperrider, D. L. (2000). *Apprreciative inquiry. Rethinking human organization toward a positive change of theory*. Champaign: Stipes.

Eakin, P. J. (1999). *How our lives become stories—making selves*. Ithaca & London: Cornell University Press.

Elbow, P. (1986). *Embracing Contraries: Explorations in Learning and Teaching*. Oxford: Oxford University Press.

Gagne, R., Briggs, L. J., & Wager, W. W. (1992). *Principles of instructional design*. Orlando: Harcourt Brace.

Halbwachs, M. (1992). *On collective memory*. The University of Chicago Press, Translated from: *Les cadres sociaux de la mémoire*.

Halsall, R. et al. (1998). *Teacher Research and School Improvement: Opening Doors From the Inside*. Buckingham: Open University Press.

Hüseyin Özer Website. (2014).

Lamarque, P. (2009). *The Philosophy of Literature*. London: Blackwell.

MacIntyre, A. (1981). *After virtue*. Notre Dame: University of Notre Dame.

Martin, H., & Ohmann, R. (1963). *The logic and rhetoric of exposition*. New York: Holt, Rinehart & Winston.

Meeks, T. W., & Jeste, D. V. (2009). Neurobiology of wisdom: a literature overview. *Archives of General Psychiatry, 66*(4), 355–365.

Merriam, S. B., Caffarella, R., & Baumgartner, L. (2007). *Learning in adulthood: a comprehensive guide*. San Francisco: Jossey-Bass.

Mumford, L. (1970). *The myth of the machine (two volumes)*. San Diego: Harcourt, Brace, Jovanovich.

Raine, C. (1998). Review of Peter Davidson's complete works of george orwell: socialist, imperialist, down, but not out. 1 August, *Financial Times*.

Ryan, K., & Jenkins, C. (1997). On the loose—an interview with Robert Coles. *Journal of Education, 179*(3), 1–15.

Swales, M. (1978). *The German Bildungsroman from Wieland to Hesse*. Princeton: Princeton University Press.

Tiernan, P. & O'Kelly, J. (2014). Blending work and learning: the impact of a workplace learning programme on the low-skilled and long term unemployed. *Industrial and Commercial Training*, 46(7), 406–414.

Trilling, L. (1955). *The opposing self—nine essays in criticism*. Ann Arbor: University of Michigan.

Verbos, A. K., & Humphries, M. (2014). A native american relational ethic: an indigenous perspective on teaching human responsibility. *Journal of Business Ethics, 123*, 1–9. (Springer).

Chapter 6
Developing Criticality Through Reading Novels

Sometimes, immersed in his books, there would come to him the awareness of all that he did not know, of all that he had not read; and the serenity for which he laboured was shattered as he realized the little time he had in life to read so much, to learn what he had to learn.

—John Edward Williams, *Stoner*

First place, we ought to insist that folks call us 'realtors' and not 'real-estate men'. Sounds more like a reg'lar profession. Second place—What is it distinguishes a profession from a mere trade, business, or occupation? What is it? Why, it's the public service and the skill, the trained skill, and the knowledge and, uh, all that, whereas a fellow that merely goes out for the jack, he never considers the—public service and trained skill and so on. Now as a professional…

—Sinclair Lewis, *Babbitt*

Abstract This chapter concerns individual students who come from a range of professions including coaching, teaching, environmental work, the police service, dog training, the maritime industry, airlines and charities. I encourage students to explore how their life histories have made an impact on their professional growth. In doing so, I suggest that they resist simplistic answers and instead try to embrace the complexity of their lived experience and question their previous assumptions while narrating their "stories". I encourage them to use knowledge from a range of academic disciplines in a reflective way: my hypothesis is that reflective thought, properly guided, will foster change in terms of increased academic confidence. Furthermore, motivating students to read literature can help them become better communicators as they reflect on how fictional character—George Babbitt, John Stoner, Travis from *Old Yeller*—navigate the knotty issues and complex problems of life and work: reading novels is conducive to developing criticality. The students' own testimony and work appear to suggest that learning and literature complement each other: stories enrich our lives and help us to interpret and understand others.

© The Author(s) 2016
C.A. Eastman, *Improving Workplace Learning by Teaching Literature*,
SpringerBriefs in Education, DOI 10.1007/978-3-319-29028-7_6

Introduction

My final chapter differs from the previous four because it concerns the individual students with whom I have worked since 2011 at the Institute of Work Based Learning at Middlesex University. They are completing or have completed Masters degrees or Professional Doctorates and come from a range of professions including coaching, teaching, environmental work, police services, dog training, maritime and airline industries and charities.[1] The students are at the top of their professions, either managing their own businesses, directing publicly or privately owned organisations or working in a capacity to influence policy, organisational direction and professional knowledge in a specific field. The other difference is that the students from Toshiba, Wembley, Sofra and the Halifax were pursuing undergraduate certificates or diplomas. The students here have been working at a considerably advanced level at which I expect them to look at their work as critically as possible. The term "critical" is used to describe "culture, language and participation as issues of power in need of critique with the intent of emendation or alteration in the direction of social justice and participatory democracy" (Moss 2004, p. 359). Within the milieu of the narrative research students are expected to undertake, "critical" signifies the study of the relationships of power in work.

I encourage students to explore how their life histories have made an impact on their professional growth. In doing so, I suggest that they resist simplistic answers and instead try to embrace the complexity of their lived experience, examining their observations, interpretations and biases as explicitly as possible. They are expected to question their previous assumptions while narrating their "stories". As with the cohort-based students, I encourage them to use knowledge from a range of academic disciplines in a reflective way: my contention is that reflective thought, properly guided, will foster change in terms of increased academic confidence. Furthermore, motivating the students to read literature can help them to become better communicators as they reflect on how a fictional character navigates the knotty issues and complex problems of work and life: reading novels is conducive to developing criticality. The chapter that follows concerns individual postgraduate students: I see my role as encouraging criticality, which aims at questioning one's assumptions. I urge them to reflect on the life of a fictional character, a process I argue is conducive to developing criticality in real life. A common theme emerges in these students' experience: there is a discernible transformative impact from the reading of literature on the way they conceptualise their working practice.

---

[1] Both the Masters and Professional Doctorates require students to complete a negotiated work based learning project invariably taken at the end of a course of study: a student may have some accredited work as well as a project proposal module. The project is intended to improve or inform areas of the student's work/practice.

The Value of Participation

I am the module leader for postgraduate projects, which means that I oversee the VLE activities and comments, field all general questions and run five workshops virtually per term. The students begin study with me after having had their programme proposal assessed and approved. This study is a 12,000 word project which examines an aspect of their practice. Most of the students have followed a programme of specific modules which ends in this final project module—the culmination of their MA or MSc in Professional Practice. When I took over leadership of the module in 2011 I was concerned that the students' work lacked criticality or a robust inquiry into the power relationships inherent in every organisation; an appropriate depth of reflection; evidence of habitual examination of practice; and clear communication skills of which foremost was the ability to write persuasively and coherently. I therefore developed the workshops accordingly, focusing on getting students to examine these areas and post their drafts on the VLE for both their colleagues and I to make comments. Below is a sample exchange from last term which offers a flavour of how the students interact[2]:

From John:

> Here is the first draft of my second chapter. It is incomplete and has two sections which need to be added. I have had to spend a long time editing and refining down. There is so much to take from the literature and selecting what is relevant and rejecting what is superfluous has proved harder than I thought. In the end I have largely cut out the peripheral things and focussed on what has really guided and informed my study. All comments gratefully received.

From Shane:

> The chapter was impressive on two counts. 1. The accuracy and ability to move from one detailed literature reading to the next, comparing and then building on larger perspectives; 2. Whilst detail and depth were explored, your style incorporated a personal view – the writing is warm and perceptive, inviting the reader to share and read. Something I think could be improved is framing the chapter more explicitly (explaining what you set out to do at the beginning and explaining what you've done at the conclusion), however I think the chapter is excellent. In truth, I was sort of nervous about reading your chapter because the subject has the risk of losing me. Your descriptions, your insight, your story made the piece flow well and you gave your research clear contextual evidence. Your obvious passion for your work and for looking at work creatively shines through.

Students' posts are in this vein. There is a great deal of praise and support for each other, and there is invariably constructive criticism and observations on areas students think something could be clarified or improved. The essential aspect of reading each other's chapters and excerpts is that students discover that their writing either comes across clearly or does not to others who are not working in the same field of work. Unlike the industry-based cohorts with whom I have worked, these

---

[2]John was a UK university administrator and Shane the director of a coaching company in South Africa.

students cannot resort to short-hand or company jargon to make themselves under-stood: the onus on them is to make every aspect of their practice clear to a "lay-person".

Shane asks Rita, an HE lecturer in the creative industries for further clarification and suggests some refinements:

> I like your clear headings and lay out of your chapter. An interesting quandary—wanting to add technology to the communication arts and recognising the negative impact it could potentially have on communication. I do think you need to temper your writing with more academic framing—hard for a creative, I know! Whilst your familiar approach makes for relaxed reading, the data can carry less weight. One last comment—you tend to use the words "very" and "much"—generally they are not needed and detract from your argument. Oh, and a tiny observation about your references: bracketing dates after the author are followed by a full stop.

In this sometimes daunting quest to generate new knowledge, knowledge that is critical, reflective and self-aware, a community of learning can not only keep the students energised and enthusiastic about their projects, it can make perhaps what remains concealed, visible.

I had asked Shane if he would take on the responsibility of student representative. Every term I ask a particularly active student if he or she wants to volunteer for this role. The role is to feedback to the Institute examples of good practice on the course and to gather students' comments about their experience. It can also be a way of reinforcing sound pedagogic practices. Shane—and other representatives—tended to reinforce the points I made during the workshops, which made "visible" what might get lost in the herculean endeavour of producing a 12,000 word enquiry with a full time job limiting reflection, research and writing time. Shane's comments on Leila's draft exemplify how information and learning mislaid, forgotten or concealed become visible:

> Watch for over-long sentences. You are brimming with ideas but need to separate them out more. One useful thing would be to get a friend or colleague to read the work through to catch typos and suggest minor corrections. More so, as our compressed time will create rougher paragraphs. Certainly that's what's happening with my work!

A small yet important suggestion like this reinforced by one student to another can be ignored when it originates from the tutor. As the students form into a cohesive group, they begin to take on the characteristics of a productive, democratically func-tioning community of practice: they are helpful, polite, constructively critical and highly supportive of each other. They display a degree of wisdom, a wisdom medi-ated by the values of achieving a common good, in this case, a common good for the group, for the course's community of practice. Robert Sternberg, in his study into the nature of wisdom, views this wisdom as a kind of "balanced" wisdom in which people will balance "various self-interests" (intra-personal) with the interests of others (inter-personal) and of other aspects in the context of which one lives (extra-personal). Wisdom also involves creativity in that the wise solution to a problem may be far from obvious (2004, p. 152).

When I read over their posts to each other, I am particularly struck by the effort they make for each other in identifying creative ways to resolve problems. To provide a recent example, a student involved in dog obedience and training responded to an offshore maritime worker's request for feedback on his project proposal:

> My only real comment is that the scope seems quite large (to alter the course of maritime training in two Caribbean islands) and I wonder whether you could instead focus on one or two specific areas of maritime training, whilst at the same time recognising the need for other areas to be developed too. So whatever you decide to work on for this project, maybe this could be the pilot programme for something then to take into further areas. It would mean that your project could cover the whole subject but your development work could concentrate on one segment to get a greater depth and quality.

An FE teacher, Clare, added:

> It would be good to have a bit of background on you and your professional role to get a feel for the personal motivation you may have.

Derek, the offshore mariner, responded enthusiastically to the feedback, pointing out how few mariners were in the tertiary and skills training fields in this Caribbean region, and that both fellow students' suggestions were much appreciated. Although from at times widely disparate fields, the students are able to form a community of practice, which helps them to reinforce criticality and reflection for each other. In his peroration on how to help students learn more, Elbow (1986) maintains that the principle behaviour of teachers is to see students as "smart and capable". This kind of positive teacher expectation increases student learning:

> Even though we are not wholly peer with our students, we can still be peer in the crucial sense of also being engaged in learning, seeking, and being incomplete. Significant learning requires change, inner readjustments, willingness to let go. We can increase the chances of our students being willing to undergo the necessary anxiety involved in change if they see we are also willing to undergo it. (pp. 149–50).

To encourage students to form a community of practice in order to critique each other's work is part of what Elbow terms a "willingness to let go" on the part of the tutor. Allowing the peers to engage in the process of learning (and teaching) emboldens students and increases their confidence. As part of the peer-led process, telling one's story is a useful way of approaching the 12,000 word project. A recent post from Samir confirmed my belief that conceiving the project as one's story provides the richness, complexity and reflexivity necessary in a work based learning inquiry:

> During the last workshop I realised that my story is the culmination, so far, of my life's work. When I was advised to write my story and think of the report as writing my journey, life seemed suddenly clearer.

As I explained, these postgraduate work based learning students are employed in a variety of fields yet the common denominator is that they use their work as the basis for their reflective inquiry. Work has been so integrated into their lives, their stories become stories of their working lives and how they arrived at their professional junctures, what politics they have had to manage, what passions and determinations have compelled them to carry on, what perplexities they have experienced, and what frustrations and confusions they have surmounted.

It is crucial that students participate fully as a community of learning: I have found that these "community principles" produce engaged and deep learning. Elbow (1986, p. 13) explains how this way of learning is so much more fruitful than from students "feeding back undigested ideas from lectures and reading". If Elbow is right, it follows that no one learns by being fed information. I observed that fostering the ability to apply new concepts by getting the students to become immersed in each other's work increases real learning significantly.

I then began to think that if students seemed to understand their own project concepts so much better by engaging with their fellow students' work, it would be even more beneficial if they would examine "a story" within the realm of their practice. Elbow reminds us that "we often think best by telling stories" (p. 146), and, by extension, we often think best by reading stories. I would suggest that reading stories is an equally potent means of fostering thinking and reflective practice. I therefore reasoned that it would be profitable for students to look at novels that examine the tensions between work and society and to explore works that explore the competing conflicts within business and society in order to see how literature could teach them about how to live and specifically how to balance tensions between work and life.

Babbitt: New Ways to See the World

I introduced Sinclair Lewis' *Babbitt* (1922) into the project syllabus. *Babbitt* is the story of George Babbitt, a prosperous partner at a real estate firm, who represents a man beset by social delusions nurtured by his consumerist, conformist environment:

> To George F. Babbitt, as to most prosperous citizens of Zenith, his motor-car was poetry and tragedy, love and heroism. The office was his pirate ship but the car his perilous excursion ashore (Lewis 2006 p. 34).

Yet there is a niggling anxiety that all is not right and he comes to doubt the conventions of middle-class society and to despise his conformist life: "Mechanical religion—a dry, hard church, shut off from the real life of the streets, inhumanly respectable as a top-hat. Mechanical golf and dinner-parties and bridge and conversation." (p. 34)

He has an epiphany that his life has been defined by a lack, a sadness:

> He saw the years, the brilliant winter days and all the long sweet afternoons which were meant for summery meadows, lost in such brittle pretentiousness. He thought of telephoning about leases, of cajoling men he hated, of making business calls and waiting in dirty ante-rooms – hat on knee, yawning at fly-specked calendars, being polite to office-boys. 'I don't hardly want to go back to work,' he prayed. 'I'd like to — I don't know." But he was back next day, busy and of doubtful temper. (p. 227).

Babbitt needs—and as readers, we become aware Sinclair Lewis wants him—to break out of his social, economic and psychological cul de sac. He revolts against society, defiantly drinking too much, rejecting his clubby respectability and carrying on with a mistress. The ending is ambiguous. A superficial reading of the novel might suggest that Babbitt relapses into his old bullying, conformist ways. Neither I nor my students were so convinced.

Two intrepid coaching students took up the challenge of reading this thick tome replete with turn of the 20th century American slang ("Rats, what's the odds?"), casual racism ("coon", "kike") and an especially difficult eponymous anti-hero described by one of the students Louis as "a pompous, self-satisfied windbag, who, in the end, started disconcertingly to remind me of myself". The other student Nanette thought of him as "everyman, a lesson for us all." I thought that Nanette, a Black South African woman who was investigating the coaching needs of women in leadership roles within a major African charity, would be particularly repulsed by George Babbitt, yet ironically, she told me that she loved the novel and found many striking parallels between the early 20th century American fictionalised town of Zenith and modern, cosmopolitan Johannesburg. In fact, she discerned:

> Babbitt's world as a mirror image of my own world in Johannesburg – the sad and key similarity between the two worlds is society punishing and reprimanding those who dare to be different, those who dare to live an authentic life. Throughout the novel there is an obsession with long descriptions of non-essentials such as the look, feel and cost, for instance, of a cigarette lighter, people's clothing and the interior decor of offices. It struck me that this is so typical of my world: one's social status is determined not so much by what they give to the community but by the job they do, the clothes they wear, the car they drive and the circles of friends and networks they are seen with. The book could easily be set in modern day Johannesburg.

Superficially, Nanette's investigation into the spheres of influence of women in southern Africa, especially examining African women in leadership positions on the continent, seems so far removed from the small town American concerns of the 1920s, that attempting to make a rewarding comparison between the two entities appears fruitless, even ridiculous. However, notwithstanding Nanette's observation that the two seemingly polarised societies share striking similarities, she was more interested in Lewis' use of George Babbitt as a character to address the issue of a mechanised and socialised conformity in office and professional life, as well as the author's use of Babbitt to explore the idea of the "true self".

As a coach, Nanette was concerned with people's professional performances and the obstacles that might impinge on these performances. Her in-depth investigation into leadership research and theories established a nexus between coaching and leadership performance. She found a paucity of research on women's leadership in Africa and, in order to close that gap, she undertook a large scale investigation into corporate coaching in Africa, positing the need to come up with creative solutions to recruit and retain effective women leaders in an area in which 76 % of young women between the ages of 15 and 24 were affected by HIV and AIDS (Dube 2009). Babbitt's gradual questioning of his existence within the pressures of his "corporate" life captured Nanette's imagination because of her long professional commitment to helping her clients embrace the vitality and autonomy of their true selves. She observes:

Babbitt realises he is not the best paid or most successful real estate professional and neither are his dinners the most talked about. There is an ever-present feeling of being lesser than the next person which drives him to spend money he does not have to keep up with people who do not care about him. His relationships are not real and they are certainly not beneficial to him (although he wants to believe they are). And so is the vanity and tragedy of the professionals of my world today. Work and busyness seem to have taken over people's lives and yet there seems to be no satisfaction with the quality of their lives. It is as if the professional has *become* the life, instead of being a tool towards living a satisfactory life. For me, the major lesson of *Babbitt* is to be cognizant of the price and cost of swimming against the tide and the need to find out who you really are. Lewis is suggesting that there is a price for being authentic…and the question is – how much are we willing to pay to be able to find ourselves?

At the outset of the novel George Babbitt accepts the repressive and superficially comforting conformism around him because the alternative would be too painful: the autonomy of self is a place that is difficult to reach and a lonely space in which to reside. Nanette could see that Babbitt was flailing about, questioning his existence, attempting to connect with the vitality of his true self, yet falling short. Louis, another coaching student, was repulsed by the character whom he identified as a "ghastly coward". However, there was still a transformative experience aesthetically, if not philosophically:

Sinclair Lewis' prose style is enviable. It was a superb exercise for me to examine how he constructed his sentences, how he persuaded me that this world he created really existed. I am usually exposed to a specific way of writing which I will call "bureaucratease". I don't usually read novels so this was hard going for me. But looking at the mechanics of the language enhanced my learning. I may have felt that the character was delusional, even obnoxious, but the way Lewis wrote about his hypocrite was a total joy. I am far more careful in how I construct my language and pay more attention to the words I choose now.

In this testimonial, the power of reading as a means of facilitating better student writing emerges. Using novels, therefore, not only helps students to visualise strong and elegant prose, but encourages the virtue of inter-disciplinary exploration. The world is not organised into disciplines and examining a problem within the confines of a single discipline reveals very little about that problem. I am convinced that the artificial boundaries between disciplines hinder rather than enhance student learning by restricting learning to compartmentalised modes of inquiry. In fact, as Barzun (1989) points out, specialists can often breed specialist readers. He offers the example of an American Civil War specialist reading nothing but American Civil War military history and contends that when we focus on a single topic, it does not enhance our vision but is instead self-limiting. Louis admitted that most of his reading had been confined to what he called "coaching literature", which may or may not include paragons of excellent writing styles but did nevertheless confine him to a specialist area. Reading *Babbitt* exposed him to a very different type of work, which equipped him, by his own admission, with sensitivity to and an appreciation of the mechanics of language. Barzun suggests rather contentiously that specialism creates an obsession with facts and that we should strive to mine instead the depth and breadth of the humanities:

> We cry aloud for 'communication' and say we suffer from the lack of it. We ought instead to demand conversation which pedants so seldom achieve. For conversation is the principle of the good society and the good life. It is the key to the prison cells of our professions, our vocations, and our hobbies (p. 119).

Barzun's rallying cry for dialogue, for reflection, for challenging through questions reminds me of Nanette's observation of her fellow Johannesburg colleagues as being preoccupied with work and business to the detriment of the quality of their lives. Novels such as *Babbitt* help to create that communication, that dialogue between reader and text, that reflection on one's own life, which could be considered an essential aspect of a cultivated mind. In imagining one's way into the world of a fictional character, students can find new ways to see the world and new ways to reflect on the pressures and values of corporate, managerial life through a different lens. As Louis pointed out, the advantage alone in examining the prose style of a great writer—leaving aside the way a novel like *Babbitt* can trigger responses that help students to assess and discriminate between alternative opinions and views—is invaluable. He remarks on the following passage:

> It was coming to him that perhaps all life as he knew it and vigorously practised it was futile; that heaven as portrayed by the Reverend Dr. John Jennison Drew was neither probable nor very interesting; that he hadn't much pleasure out of making money; that it was of doubtful worth to rear children merely that they might rear children who would rear children. What was it all about? What did he want? (Lewis 2006, p. 263).

> We learn from Maslow's Hierarchy of Needs about people's values, and many theorists have definitive positions on intrinsic and extrinsic motivation. How refreshing it is to have a great prose stylist encapsulate the concept of needs and motivation within the crossroads of general ennui and confusion about life that most of us face at some point in our lives.

Since the majority of work based learning students are located in organisations in which technical knowledge is viewed at a premium, they have not had the opportunity to reflect on the practical skills—those complex, interpretative and discursive practices—that are developed by the study of literature.

In John Carey's (2005) controversial *What Good Are the Arts?*, he reports on a study conducted in 2003 at a young offenders unit in Durham in which a group of boys, naturally resistant to reading, were introduced to Golding's *Lord of the Flies*. They made astonishing breakthroughs in their recognition that their anger had led them to acts, at times, of thorough barbarism. Carey concludes simply "I am not disputing the educational potential of other arts, but I do not believe that *any other art than literature* could have produced these results" (2005, p. 212, my italics). Carey's experience is similar to the experiences of Nanette and Louis. In fact, in Louis' work with young people as both a coach and mentor, he thought that exposing his clients to literary texts just might be the trigger for the transformational experience they needed. Using literary texts to get students to reflect on their options and methods of thinking—to harness their own innate wisdom—we can help students to reflect on the choices in their lives as well as help them to deconstruct ideas and texts in order to deal with complexity and ambiguity.

The Loneliness of the Lecturer—*Stoner*

John Edward Williams' *Stoner* is the story of a college teacher in the Midwest between the two world wars. The eponymous hero, Stoner, is a lonely man whose job, in the author's words, "gave him a particular kind of identity and made him what he was" (Barnes 2013). The book is about work—the work of raising a child in a dysfunctional household, the work of teaching literature to unyielding students, the work of surviving each day in a politically charged, antagonistic university atmosphere. My rationale for introducing it to two students, one a teacher, the other an ex-teacher and now a coach, Catherine and Penelope, was that their pedagogical concerns—disaffected students, bureaucratic exigencies, dogmatic regimes— seemed uncannily similar to Stoner's at his Midwest university in the 1920s. Catherine told me that being exposed to American literature gave her an opportunity to widen her horizons, and, in particular, reading *Stoner* helped her to develop her voice:

> I suddenly realised what the hell this doctorate was about because I was freed up and inspired to write [by looking at literature]. The literature has really built my confidence particularly in areas where I felt really de-skilled and it has helped me write in a much more creative way.

Literary works provide clarity on a number of issues. For Nussbaum (2010), such works offer enlightenment on moral dilemmas. A social historian might derive rich information from an eighteenth century novel that demonstrates contemporary attitudes. A philologist would profit from a linguistically innovative work in a modernist style. Freudians might admire works in which the unconscious can be discerned (Lamarque 2009). For Catherine, Williams' work rewarded her attention by supporting her to write in a more creative way. If we accept that learning and knowledge are valuable, and that reading literary works contributes to attaining knowledge, we can see how Catherine's inspiration was triggered by imaginative and limpid prose.

I asked Penelope if she could relate what Williams said once in an interview— "The important thing in the novel to me is Stoner's sense of a job…a job in the good and honourable sense of the word. His job gave him a particular kind of identity and made him what he was" (Barnes 2013)—to her own job and she answered:

> My job defines me as a successful, independent woman. As a business owner, I am respected. Stoner echoes my sentiments when he says to his lover "We would be nothing" in response to her suggestion that they leave their respective jobs [to escape small town university gossip]. I reflected on what I would be if I gave up my business to take up a more secure job for the sake of my daughter. Of course it would be better to have her mom around more and better for me to have less stress. But it would leave me feeling as though I had nothing if I didn't have my business which is my identity. I really felt I was in the presence of wisdom reading *Stoner* (2012). The author completely understood the feeling of completeness and fulfilment when you find your true religion – the job that doesn't feel a job but a calling.

Williams' *Stoner* is fictionalised, but fictionality, as Lamarque (2009, p. 239) observes is "no bar to the advancement or illustration of worldly truth". From her response could we deduce that Penelope has learned something valuable from reading *Stoner*? Writers have long maintained that we can learn how to understand better human nature through literature. Penelope's equating her strong sense of identity as an educator and coach with Stoner's sense of nullity beyond his role as a professor of literature is powerful. Penelope's investigation into developing professional people through coaching has been strengthened by her engagement with literature. Readers may not believe something differently but their way of seeing the world can be affected. Penelope used *Stoner* to reflect on what she perceived as a less than successful teaching experience at a private school in South Africa:

> I was saddened and surprised that my enthusiasm for the work I did as well as my passion for learning and teaching was not shared by most of the students. Very few appreciated or took advantage of the wonderful opportunity that they had to learn and grow. When reading *Stoner*, I felt a strong connection to him. I had not realised [before reading about his disappointment with his disengaged students] how significant this sadness and disappointment was in changing my life. Unlike Stoner, I did not persevere in teaching those students – those who didn't want to learn. I chose to teach and grow people in my company as well as in Women for Afrika – willing learners.

Penelope has been able to transfer her teaching skills and love of learning to her own business in which being creative is valued. Creativity, to me, is supporting students to understand human nature by exploring literature. Stoner's life felt real to the students because they were able to imagine him creatively. Similarly, when we as educators, feel constrained to follow a rigid syllabus, which allows no means to be creative, we become dull and ossified. At times I have been overwhelmed by the preponderance of business related books and journals on a suggested reading list for work based learning students. I have no particular criticism of the proliferation of "learning models" and "business models", but we need to offer students a generous inventory of reading materials including literary works. As Peter Elbow admonishes, we need to call into question intellectual disciplinary divisions and "adjust our picture of what is natural in learning and teaching" (1986, p. xiii). His argument is that curricular changes can increase real learning, and significantly that real learning comes only when we understand a concept so well it becomes a part of us. This idea has profound implications in improving workplace learning by teaching literature.

My Life as a Dog: *Old Yeller*

I had a group of canine specialists over two terms, one working with dogs in the London Metropolitan police service and the others running their own canine behavioural businesses. I asked them to read Gipson's 1956 classic *Old Yeller* about a dog who changes the life of a family living in the late nineteenth century in the Texas wilderness because I wanted to gauge how reading fiction could influence their projects: I wanted a book to provide a "medium so that [they could] interrogate human intentions" (Lamarque 2009, p. 197), and, especially for them, canine behaviour. Lamarque is convinced that when we read fiction we supplement our reflections on the characters' motives from our own experiences. Donna, whose project investigated the interactions between dogs and humans in order to support her clients to understand their canine charges better, observed that *Old Yeller* subverted the usual literary depiction between man and dog:

> I saw the 'yellow dog' [Old Yeller] as a Labrador, presenting an immediate similarity to my project which investigates behaviour and emotion in the Labrador. I was expecting yet another story of an unrealistic human-dog relationship where the dog demonstrates impossible feats of emotional compassion. Instead the book is a compelling account of the author's understanding of the human-dog relationship and provides real insight into this interaction. The story portrays real life survival struggles for both the family and Old Yeller. It is an account of a successful human-dog relationship with an unbreakable bond developed through trust, loyalty and understanding. There is a lot that domestic dog owners and professionals could learn from reading this book: appreciating a clear relationship between two species, both respecting each other's boundaries, developing a healthy and productive emotional bond, and focusing on what people thought appropriate for a time and situation.

Lamarque correctly states that it would be irrational not to feel emotions towards fictional characters: Donna admitted that the book was a "tear-jerker". To feel emotion is a proper response to a tragic situation. Moreover, engaging imaginatively with fictional characters and situations—to adopt the view of a fictional character—highlights the importance of how learners need to rediscover and recreate their own meaning. It is the inferior model of learning that views learning as a process that transmits material from teacher to student. Reading fiction encourages students to adopt a particular stance. The use of stories, for example, has been growing in momentum over the past few years within the study of law. Applied legal storytelling is the practice of using stories and their symbolism to explore better ways of telling the client's story (McPeake and Ashford 2014, pp. 137–139). Fictional discourse is certainly not "incompatible" with the truth:

> No one could dispute that readers can learn about the real world from fiction: they pick up facts about history, geography, points of etiquette, clothing and fashions, idiomatic usage, as well as how to perform practical tasks, how people behave in certain situations. What it is like to be in an earthquake, a storm at seam or a blazing house. Fiction is often a vehicle for teaching even outside the normal literary context (Lamarque 2009, pp. 221–222).

Do the students attach value to this learning? Liam, the owner of a dog obedience practice and a practitioner in canine behaviour for many years, pointed out that there were a number of events in *Old Yeller* that highlighted innate canine behaviour and had solid implications for the human-canine relationship. At the beginning of the story, Old Yeller, a seemingly stray dog, wanders into the Texan homestead of the family of a mother, the 14 year old narrator and his 8 year old brother and "steals" a large piece of meat hanging up outside, waiting to be cured. Liam commented:

> Travis [the narrator] assumes that the dog should feel guilty which typifies people's lack of knowledge about animals. A dog doesn't feel guilty and in effect must be caught in the act within two seconds if it is to be reprimanded. The learning for dog owners is to treat such an incident as natural and then investigate ways of moderating their dog's behaviour with simple commands. The average dog owner would probably not know this. In fact, there are a number of events in *Old Yeller* that can be extracted to highlight typical canine behaviour.

I then asked Liam if reading *Old Yeller* had enriched his investigation into canine behavioural modification:

> My personal preference has been to read factual books regarding canine training, and behaviour and all previous canine related modules have been down this avenue. I now believe that reading *Old Yeller* has enabled me to reflect in another way. It should assist me to become a better canine psychologist not only because [the book] reiterates canine behaviour but it allowed me *to interpret* human responses to the canine and interactions between human and canine (my italics).

Liam was not moved, or certainly did not report being moved, by the aesthetic considerations of Gipson's canine classic. The story was of singular interest to him not as a work of art but as an exercise in interpretation. As readers, we supply our own connections between our lives and the story: our reflections on characters can originate from our own lives so that a story such as *Old Yeller* can provide "a medium" for us to "interrogate human intentions" (Lamarque 2009, p. 197). Liam used the verbs "reiterate" and "interpret" unselfconsciously: not only was he able to engage imaginatively with these fictional characters in their fictional situations, he was able to draw generalisations and even truths about the nature of humans and that of dogs and the nature of the relationship between humans and dogs. Liam did not need to pick up facts about the "real world" of human and canine interactive behaviour from reading *Old Yeller*: he was already an experienced canine psychologist. What was instructive to me in his reading of the book was the *value* he attached to his learning. The value for Liam was a confirmation of the "truth" he perceived in his own observations of humans and dogs over the years.

Iris Murdoch makes a significant point about how literature highlights human nature with startling clarity:

> 'Truth' is something we recognise in good art when we are led to a juster, clearer, more detailed, more refined understanding. Good art 'explains' truth itself, by manifesting deep conceptual connections. Truth is clarification, justice, compassion (1992, p. 321).

Pete, a canine specialist and trainer, working for a UK police service, relates his reading experience of *Old Yeller*:

> Literature can enrich projects, reports, investigating even sales pitches. It humanises stuffy accounts that people speed read and forget. It is an exciting and animated instructor who can bring enthusiasm for a subject into the classroom. Literature can assist in sparking the imagination and providing more personal descriptive pictures to the teaching process.

All three canine specialists were convinced by Gipson's portrayal of a stray dog who ends up protecting a family in the outback and, more crucially, they discerned connections between the book and their own learning. The students also read an academic article that interrogates "the multiple and ambiguous representations of the dog—this most prevalent and successfully integrated of our animal-others" (Williams 2007, p. 92).

Williams' article is a detailed depiction of the social and cultural roles dogs have had for humans over the centuries, taking in Carl Jung's ideas of the dog/coyote as an archetypal trickster figure, Native American canine tropes as dogs as shadowy deity figures and Egyptian and Ancient Greek representations of the dog both positive and negative. Although the students acknowledged the wealth of historical information in the article, they found themselves more critically and creatively engaged with reading the fiction of *Old Yeller*. There seemed to be, possibly because of a more *emotional* response to the work, a deeper connection to it. I am not making an exorbitant claim for the value of integrating literature into a work based learning curriculum or indeed any curriculum, but it must be acknowledged that the students have demonstrated the value that reading literature in the form of fiction has had on their work in terms of gaining insights into their practice as well as into their lives. Donna grasps this value when she points out the sang-froid displayed by the 14 year old left on the homestead in loco parentis:

> The overall control Travis has on his emotions throughout the book is exceptional. He rarely lets his emotions distract him from his goal of keeping the farm running and his family protected, despite the inward battles he has and emotional struggles he faces in his relationship with Old Yeller. This is a lesson we could all learn to help us in day to day life – not to conceal emotion but to control it and release it through appropriate channels. All society would benefit from this.

Stories, our own and others', have the potential to become narratives by which we can develop our own disciplines and lives more fully.

The Value of Literature

In 2014 I sent out 20 questionnaires to and also interviewed a half dozen students who had just finished or were still engaged in their project work. I found the responses germane to my research and will examine the overarching themes here. My primary question was if the "interdisciplinary elements", particularly reading fiction and non-fiction, I had introduced into their course of study had had any effect on their learning. A corollary of this question was if their course reading had improved their writing skills. Sean, a coach who was working with a group of women in Saudi Arabia, reported back to me that the interdisciplinary reading had:

> an enormous effect. You had suggested an article by Camille Paglia ('Junk Bonds and Corporate Raiders: Academe in the Hour of the Wolf'), a feminist article that I didn't see an initial place for. But because I didn't see an initial place for it, it gave me the opportunity to recognise something that I wasn't even vaguely aware of. [The article and this realisation] had a huge impact on my learning and on my writing and afterwards on my professional application. I see [Paglia] as the voice of the crone. She is very much in one's face like a cold crone, saying 'let's not beat around the bush, let's get down to it.' I'm not being harsh or disrespectful – being a 'cold crone' is a good thing – wise and direct without needing to keep to any of the social niceties. I think in our speaking and writing we spend too much time dancing around the niceties, we, and I, need to be clear and direct.

Paglia (1991) recounts the task of reviewing a book on homosexuality in ancient Athens that she deemed poorly written, which forced her to take stock of the serious issue of scholarly ethics in academia. Writing about the author and his poorly written work, she makes the following charge:

> Like most of the American academics who have wandered into sex studies [he] lacks the most elementary understanding of the basic principles of history, anthropology, and psychology necessary for such a work. The exposition of these essays is tortured, bloated, meandering, pretentious, confused (p. 171).

Paglia clearly refrains from observing any of Sean's idea of "social niceties". Naturally Paglia is writing literary criticism, which has its own principles, aesthetics and considerations, far removed from a postgraduate work based learning project exploring canine behaviour tendencies or maritime law challenges or engineering issues at UK ports. Her directness and her ability to make her analysis relevant, critical and bold, however, influenced Sean's writing style in terms of how his final project appeared: what impact it had and what was salient in it. By his own admission, Sean's writing style was at first meandering and less than diligent in expressing what he wanted to say. Like many students I have taught on this project course, he had an over-reliance on adjectives and adverbs. Before students learn to be critical in their arguments, they tend to be munificent in the sprinkling of descriptive words in an attempt to convey meaning. To a certain extent, we, as educators, need to instil a mode of trained literary discernment in our students. This need not necessarily be delivered by reading literary works but can be instilled by reading essays that demonstrate insight and erudition delivered with the kind of clarity students can emulate.

Gilbert, an engineering student who was investigating safety issues at UK ports, commented on what he perceived as my technique for persuading students to shift from a descriptive style of writing to a more discursive and sinewy mode, trimmed of the superfluous modifiers and meaningless clichés:

> I would describe your method as successive. You start by giving an over-view of what is required and then we feed back to you our ideas. Then you make us focus on specific content which is valid. Then you fine tune the process, making sure we are arguing, not describing, until we create a polished gem. I got the impression that some students took this procedure as pressure, but this is a masters course and we need to pay due attention to the writing. The actual content of my work has come alive by avoiding the emotionless third person and passive voice. Now I embrace analysis whereas before, without writing guidance, my project would have ended up a standard technical report of something that cured a short-term problem. It is readable now and can be used in far more ways by a wider audience.

Gilbert explained that his previous education had been "purely technical" and that he had learned "a lot of theory". He had not been required to "translate that theory". In helping students to translate their practice and theory into clear, readable, even publishable work, I encourage them to attend carefully to how writers craft their work.

Too often students, possibly because they are so close to their subjects and professions, neglect the attention needed to explicate what their aims and objectives are, why a subject is problematic, how it will be resolved, what their methods of inquiry have revealed. Their project narratives are replete with serious and complicated issues that need to be supplemented constructively with detail and examined with a high degree of scrutiny. In order to interpret their work to their readers—me, as their assessor, their fellow peers, their work colleagues, a wider community of readers perhaps from a subsequent public dissemination of their work—why their investigation is important and how it will benefit those in their field, they must subject their writing to fairly stringent analysis.

Gilbert comments:

> Not only have I learned to be more analytical on this course, I have learned how to express this analysis in words in order to gain recognition for my achievements at work, especially my technical projects. I had to translate my hypotheses and ideas as clearly as possible. I had to thoroughly think through my ideas and then provide reasoned arguments why alternatives would not work. I think in many work places people are not so inclined to be analytical. Time and time again, I see people jump in with both feet and make mistakes which are very obvious to me. Within the engineering world the carefully worded reasoned argument has got lost.

Analysis is hardly confined to the literary world. All disciplines promote the fundamental idea in academia that a judgment that is not reinforced or substantiated is worthless. It is not only within the realm of literature and literary studies that students are encouraged or even required to weigh fundamental principles, explore conceptual connections between properties and pursue lines of thought beyond unreflective commonplaces. Because of my background in literature, I direct the masters and doctoral students to the features of literature that I believe will help them to produce excellent projects. Even with literature in the form of fiction that I encourage them to read, I do not expect them to read a novel as a work of art nor to appreciate the novel as a literary specialist.

A postgraduate degree project student is a "common reader", a term first espoused by Dr Johnson and then amplified by Virginia Woolf as someone who reads for pleasure. I want the students to derive pleasure from novels, but I also want their reading to illuminate their inquiry as well as offer them ways of writing with attentiveness, as Sean amply illustrated with his engagement with Camille Paglia. Above all, I attempt to promote the value of literary works. If we accept that learning and knowledge are valuable, then "[a]ttaining knowledge, overcoming ignorance, and learning about ourselves and the world are among the highest aspirations of the human mind, enshrined in education and science" (Lamarque 2009, p. 255).

The literary works that the students access—essays by Camille Paglia, novels by Sinclair Lewis, Fred Gipson, and John Edward Williams, and ones I discuss further on such as those by Antoine Saint-Exupery and Richard Henry Dana—do not have to be useful or have an educative factor, yet students find reading them rewarding. As Sean reminded me:

> I have not been a prolific reader. It has been a weakness and a gap. I have probably read more in the last year [during the project course] than I have read in the past twenty years. So that says something. My ability to attend to what in a book has weight or relevance has markedly improved. In the past I banked largely on my opinions because not being a prolific reader, I had to. It can be incredibly empowering to see that there are so many

assets outside of my own mind. When something comes up now, I tend to weigh it. I am more specific about how I use words.

Concluding Remarks: Silver Wings into the Heavens and Full Mast into the Wind

Michael, an aviation engineer and part-time pilot, read *Vol de Nuit* (*Night Flight*), Antoine de Saint-Exupéry's story of the early airmail service in 1930s Argentina. The protagonist, Riviere, wants to see aircraft used in preference to the well-established shipping and railroad services of the day to deliver mail. In order to make this cost-effective, pilots must fly at night, and night flying holds an array of dangers. One of Riviere's pilots, Fabien, decides to continue his flight in a storm despite the very real possibility of death. I asked Michael if *Vol de Nuit* supported his project:

> It forced me into examining another person's writing with a critical eye instead of accepting it as is. This is an essential skill when reviewing project literature since it stimulates the thought process and develops the ability to see one's own writing objectively. Just because I see something in a particular way does not mean others will. Reading *Vol de Nuit* (2000) with the idea of critiquing it helped me to critique my own project accordingly. The subject of "commercial awareness" is raised in the novel. Riviere would undoubtedly agree with the commercial necessities of continuing a flight instead of landing and causing delays. I feel that the choice of fiction is important. In my case I would have been less inclined to view Beckett's *Waiting for Godot* with quite the same interest as I did with *Vol de Nuit* and consequently I would struggle to relate it to my work based learning project.

Fiction portrays life journeys that include transformative experiences. Michael told me that after leaving school he never wanted to work out why an author wrote how or what he did. He was "through with" analysis of structure, composition, grammar and syntax. However, Saint-Exupéry's story interested him. He said he could relate to the story because the author demonstrated the danger of having a narrow focus to one's life:

> Riviere's benchmark was the job and this is a fickle hook upon which to hang one's life, irrespective of whether one does it for the money or the prestige. If the job goes well, you are happy. What if you lose your job? Does this mean you are less of a person? When the lights fade, and the applause dies, what is left? Only you, but then who are you?

The concept of identity not only comprises so many facets of who we are, but is an essential determinant in our relations with others, reinforced by social and cultural circumstances. Readers such as Michael are able to perceive their identity as going beyond the boundaries of their profession. As Berthe Lund and Tatiana Chemi point out: "[the] formation of human beings (Bildung) is a process that is challenging and involves a number of phenomena" (2015, ix). To identify with the formation of a fictional character can stimulate transformational learning. Lund and Chemi (2015) are concerned with the role emotions play in transformative learning, but it is not difficult to make the leap between identifying emotionally with a character and becoming a more critical self-reflector.

Omar, a sea-captain based in the Middle East, chose to read Richard Henry Dana's *Two Years Before the Mast*. I asked him if Dana's nineteenth-century work still held lessons for mariners today. He told me that the narrative provided him:

> with a real and authentic understanding of American maritime history and the major difficulties, problems and obstacles experienced by seafarers in that great age of sailing. Reading the story helped me to relate to such themes of adventure and survival in maritime life. We all have to learn how to deal with life's challenges, stresses and workloads.

He extracted a passage from the book to support his reflections:

> We must come down from our heights, and leave our straight paths, for the by-ways and low places of life, if we would learn truths by strong contrasts; and in hovels, in forecastles, and among our own outcasts in foreign lands, see what has been wrought upon our fellow creatures by accident, hardship, or strife (Dana 1869).

He observed:

> Dana's story is a microcosm of the human condition, a journey full of challenges, dangers and adventures. Dana urges us to learn from the past and, as my father always told me: he who has no past has no future. The world will keep changing and we have to make ourselves ready to accommodate such changes. A lot of the struggles and abuses of power Dana catalogues are with us today. Some people have to overcompensate in order to gain respect, and the weaknesses of captains may lead to unfairness and injustice for normal seafarers.

Omar and the other students appear to suggest that learning and literature complement each other. Stories enrich our lives and help us "to interpret and understand others" (Omar's words). There is the additional value of "exposure to rich linguistic output" according to Omar, a rich linguistic output that can enhance students' critical analysis when they, as readers, attend carefully to language. Over the years my fellow lecturers and I have struggled with the challenge of improving student writing, and my own work integrating literature into a curriculum of professional practice study has strongly suggested that students can learn to express themselves more clearly when they are attentive to the way good writers express themselves. My oft-repeated dictum "keep it simple" becomes reinforced by their reading clear prose unencumbered by dense circumlocutions, ambiguous references, clichéd business-speak and the vagaries of intellectualised jargon. Students benefit emotionally and intellectually from a gripping story, compellingly told, and it helps them to observe that they can make their own stories in the form of business plans, projects and investigations compelling.

As Omar summarises, "If Dana's story was one of smooth sailing in calm seas under the command of a fair, knowledgeable and wise captain, we would most likely never have heard the tale."

Similarly, we would have nothing to impart if our students were already experts. There is much we can learn from each other. Every student's story has added to my own bank of knowledge. I thank them for their knowledge, attentiveness, enthusiasm, and, above all, wisdom as we sail full mast into the sea of further learning adventures. If we can imagine learning as an ocean of opportunity and extend the mariner metaphor to educational pursuits, allow me to use Dana's parting words to his readers with you, my readers:

> And I will take the liberty, on parting with my reader, who has gone down with us to the ocean, and 'laid his hand upon its mane', to commend to his kind wishes, and to the benefit of his efforts, that class of men with whom, for a time, my lot was cast. I wish rather to do this, since I feel that whatever attention this book may gain, and whatever favor it may find, I shall owe almost entirely to that interest in the sea, and those who follow it, which is so easily excited in us all.

References

Barnes, J. (2013). Review of Stoner, Guardian Newspaper, 13th December.

Barzun, J. (1989). *The culture we deserve*. Middletown, Connecticut: Wesleyan University Press.

Carey, J. (2005). *What good are the arts?*. London: Faber & Faber.

Dana, R. H. (1869). *Two years before the mast*. Boston: Fields & Osgood.

Dube, S. (2009). *New debates and issues in HIV prevention* (vol. 2, no. 5). Johannesburg: Openspace, OSISA.

Elbow, P. (1986). *Embracing Contraries: explorations in learning and teaching*. New York and Oxford: Oxford University Press.

Gipson, F. (1956). *Old yeller*. Boston: Houghton Mifflin.

Lamarque, P. (2009). *The philosophy of literature*. London: Blackwell.

Lewis, S. (2006). *Babbitt*. London: Vintage Books.

Lund, B., & Chemi, T. (2015). *Dealing with emotions: A pedagogical challenge to innovative learning*. Rotterdam: Sense Publications.

McPeake, R., & Ashford, C. (2014). Editorial. *The Law Teacher, 48*(2), 137–139.

Moss, G. (2004). Provisions of trustworthiness in critical research narrative: Bridging intersubjectivity and fidelity. *The Qualitative Report, 9*(2), 359–374.

Murdoch, I. (1992). *Metaphysics as a guide to morals*. Harmondsworth: Penguin.

Nussbaum, M. (2010). *Not for profit: Why democracy needs the humanities*. Princeton, New Jersey: Princeton University Press.

Paglia, C. (1991). *Sex, art, and American culture*. New York: Vintage Books.

Saint-Exupéry, A. (2000). *Southern mail and night flight*. London: Penguin.

Sternberg, R. (2003). *Wisdom, intelligence and creativity synthesised*. Cambridge: Cambridge University Press.

Williams, J. E. (2012). *Stoner*. London: Vintage.

Williams, D. (2007). The difficulty of being a Dog. *MIT Press, 51*(1), 92–118.

Lightning Source UK Ltd.
Milton Keynes UK
UKOW06f1125101116

287325UK00005B/17/P